RETROGRADE PLANETS

Part I

JUPITER AND VENUS

notionpress
.com

RETROGRADE PLANETS

Part I

JUPITER AND VENUS

Himanshu Shangari

notionpress.com

Notion Press

Old No. 38, New No. 6

McNichols Road, Chetpet

Chennai - 600 031

First Published by Notion Press 2016

ISBN 978-93-5206-800-5

Om Namah Shivaay

This book has become possible with the Grace of Lord Shiva and each valuable word in this book is only due to his Blessings. This Book is dedicated to the advancement of awareness and study of Vedic Astrology, which in my opinion is the oldest, most accurate and most complete faith of Astrology.

Om Namah Shivaay

Contents

They Come First

After bowing to Lord Shiva, let me take this moment to thank the person who has been an influence so strong and supportive in my life that she is second only to my Lord Shiva himself. She is none other than my respected and adorable mother, **Smt. Jeewan Lata**. So much can be said about her contribution to my life and her support in making me what I am today, that a whole book can be written about it! But, I will consider her like Lord Shiva and hence move onto the next person, after bowing to her, as even an ocean of words can't describe her real contribution in my life and for this book.

Second on the list of acknowledgments is my dear and respected father **Lt. Sh. Bodh Raj Shangari**. Though he left us when I was nine only, the mere fact that he along with my mother brought me to this world, makes me indebted to him for this life as well as for many lives to come. God Bless your soul father, wherever you are! Even though you are physically not with me anymore, you have always been present in my mind, through all the sweet memories of my childhood, and you will always be.

Let me now take this opportunity to thank my dearest friend, **Sh. Yusuf Kirmani**, the person who pushed me hard to start writing books. If I have been able to write books during this time, much credit goes to him as otherwise, I may not have done it for many more years. Thanks a lot Kirmani Ji, and keep blessing me with your friendship.

Prelude

Vedic Astrology is undoubtedly the oldest and most comprehensive faith of astrology among all such faiths practiced across the globe, and whereas some of these faiths have the depth and volume of a stream, some of a river, Vedic Astrology is the Ocean which can provide resources to all these faiths and which can validate or invalidate any one of these faiths.

I have studied and researched many such faiths like Numerology, Vaastu etc. but none of them holds their ground without the support of Vedic Astrology and it is the faith which is the backbone or motherboard of all such faiths. This is what inspired me to make a carrier choice with the Ocean itself and now after years and years of this voyage; I can happily say that I made the right choice, many years back.

The fact that Vedic Astrology is the oldest among such faiths, also exposes it and makes it vulnerable to many types of corruptions and adulterations from time to time which may have come in the form of selfish additions in some of the purest Vedic Astrology scriptures or which may have resulted from misinterpretations of many important concepts of Vedic Astrology, from time to time. It is only due to such adulterations, corruptions and misinterpretations, that Vedic Astrology does not look as complete and accurate to many people interested in it, as it actually is, in this day and age.

With the Grace of Lord Shiva, I have spent years in researching various concepts of Vedic Astrology and in finding where and how much, such concepts may have been misinterpreted and what could be the possible correct interpretation of these divine concepts. And whereas in their misinterpreted forms, most such concepts of Vedic Astrology do not hold ground in real practice of astrology, almost all of them hold solid ground in their modified forms.

I have found out this fact after years of intensive research on these topics and after cross checking them with thousands of horoscopes so that they should hold ground when it comes to real life and real horoscopes instead of just reflecting on paper, and after all this effort, I can say that now they do hold ground in their modified forms.

Hence this book should be understood as an effort to create such awareness among the lovers of Vedic Astrology that this faith itself is still as complete as it was when it was born, but various misinterpretations from time to time, may have caused confusions related to many important concepts of this faith. Through this book, I have tried to create awareness about various aspects related to the concept of retrograde planets in Vedic Astrology.

This book start with an article on retrograde planets, which discusses some of the prevailing beliefs related to retrograde planets and which also deals with some interesting facts related to retrograde planets. It should be noted that out of nine planets called Navagraha in Vedic Astrology, Sun and Moon always move in forward direction and they never go retrograde, which means that they always move from Aries to Pisces and they never move back towards the sign through which they have recently passed. On the other hand, Rahu and Ketu always move backward or so to say, they are always retrograde and they always move from Pisces to Aries. However one thing is common between these two sets of planets where the first set is that of Sun and Moon whereas the second set is that of Rahu and Ketu, and that is the fact that they never move back towards the sign they have recently passed through.

Considering an example, if Sun is transiting through Scorpio towards Sagittarius in its forward motion, it means that Sun has recently passed through the previous sign Libra and it is now passing through Scorpio. As the Sun always moves in forward direction, it will only move from Scorpio to Sagittarius and it will never move back towards Libra. Similarly if Rahu is transiting through the sign of Scorpio, it means that Rahu has recently passed through Sagittarius and now it is moving from Scorpio to Libra since it moves backward from Pisces to Aries. Here again like the Sun, though Rahu is moving backward instead of moving forward, it will never go forward and start moving towards Sagittarius through which, it has recently passed.

Hence four out of nine planets among navagraha have defined patterns of movement where Sun and Moon always move forward whereas Rahu and Ketu always move backward. However the remaining five planets namely Jupiter, Venus, Mars, Mercury and Saturn exhibit dual patterns of movement, which means that they can move in forward as well as in backward direction and this is what makes them more interesting compared to Sun, Moon, Rahu and Ketu which only exhibit movement in one direction. These five planets generally move in forward direction but after a fixed period of time and for a fixed period of time, they go retrograde which means they start moving in backward direction. Once that period of time comes to an end, they start moving in forward direction again.

This dual pattern of movement exhibited by these five planets has fascinated many astrologers and researchers from time to time and they have tried to find the true meaning as well as true relevance of this concept of retrogradation of these five generally forward moving planets. As everything in this universe happens for a reason, there must be some reason why Sun and Moon move in forward direction only, Rahu and Ketu move in backward direction only and Jupiter, Venus, Mars, Mercury and Saturn move in forward as well as in backward direction. This dual movement of these five planets among navagraha is what has made some astrologers and researchers devote many years of their lives in order to find the true meaning of this concept of retrograde motion of these five planets which generally move in forward direction.

Therefore we will deal with these five planets through this book and we will see what positive or negative effects they can cause placed in different houses of a horoscope, when they go retrograde. Hence the word retrograde planets in the context of this book should only be understood as one of these five planets, which means that Rahu and Ketu which always remain retrograde are not covered in this book and hence they should not be counted when the word retrograde planets is used in this book.

This is due to the fact that Rahu and Ketu, just like Sun and Moon, exhibit only one type of behavior and hence their study is not important in this book, whereas Jupiter, Venus, Mars, Mercury and Saturn can exhibit dual behaviors, which means they can move in forward as well as in backward direction. Hence these five planets only will be considered as retrograde planets for the context of this book.

This book will be completed in two parts where the first part will deal with retrograde Jupiter and retrograde Venus whereas the second part will deal with retrograde Mars, retrograde Mercury and retrograde Saturn.

With this, I now take your permission to lead you to the book.

Lord Shiva Bless You

Himanshu Shangari

Retrograde Planets

Vedic astrology is an ocean of interesting as well as mysterious concepts and the concept of some planets among navagraha going retrograde is one of them. Retrograde generally means moving backward or going back in time and accordingly it is assumed that when a planet goes retrograde for certain period of time, instead of continuing with its forward motion, it starts moving backward. For example, all planets among navagraha except Rahu and Ketu move in forward direction which means they move from Aries to Pisces and then they repeat this cycle again and again, where the completion of this one cycle may be different for different planets. The fastest moving planet among navagraha, Moon may complete its cycle from Aries to Pisces in less than 30 days whereas the slowest to move among navagraha, Saturn may take about 30 years to complete one cycle from Aries to Pisces.

When a planet goes retrograde, instead of moving from Aries to Pisces, it starts moving from Pisces to Aries, in the opposite direction. For instance, if Saturn is transiting through Scorpio at this time, generally it will move from Scorpio to the next sign Sagittarius which means it will move from eighth sign to the ninth sign. However when it goes retrograde for a period of some months, during those months it will start moving backward from Scorpio towards the previous sign Libra, through which it has already passed recently. Hence a retrograde planet starts moving backward for a certain period of time and then it starts moving forward again which means that after moving in backward direction for some months,

Saturn in this example will start moving from Scorpio to Sagittarius, which is the forward movement of this planet.

Now that we know what a forward moving planet is and what is a backward moving planet, it is the time to know how the planets among navagraha behave when it comes to their forward as well as backward movements through various signs. Among navagraha, Sun and Moon always move in forward direction and they never go retrograde, which means that they always move from Aries to Pisces and they never move back towards the sign through which they have recently passed. On the other hand, Rahu and Ketu always move backward or so to say, they are always retrograde and they always move from Pisces to Aries. However one thing is common among these two sets of planets where the first set is that of Sun and Moon whereas the second set is that of Rahu and Ketu, and that is the fact that they never move back towards the sign they have recently passed through.

Considering an example, if Sun is transiting through Scorpio towards Sagittarius in its forward motion, it means that Sun has recently passed through the previous sign Libra and it is now passing through Scorpio. As the Sun always moves in forward direction, it will only move from Scorpio to Sagittarius and it will never move back towards Libra. Similarly if Rahu is transiting through the sign of Scorpio, it means that Rahu has recently passed through Sagittarius and now it is moving from Scorpio to Libra since it moves backward from Pisces to Aries. Here again like the Sun, though Rahu is moving backward or instead of moving forward, it will never go forward and start moving towards Sagittarius through which, it has recently passed.

Hence four out of nine planets among navagraha have defined patterns of movement where Sun and Moon always move forward whereas Rahu and Ketu always move backward.

However the remaining five planets namely Jupiter, Venus, Mars, Mercury and Saturn exhibit dual patterns of movement, which means that they can move in forward as well as in backward direction and this is what makes them more interesting compared to Sun, Moon, Rahu and Ketu which exhibit movement in one direction only. These five planets generally move in forward direction but after a fixed period of time and for a fixed period of time, they go retrograde which means they start moving in backward direction. Once that period of time comes to an end, they start moving in forward direction again.

This dual pattern of movement exhibited by these five planets has fascinated many astrologers and researchers from time to time and they have tried to find the true meaning as well as true relevance of this concept of retrogradation of these five generally forward moving planets. As everything in this universe happens for a reason, there must be some reason why Sun and Moon move in forward direction only, Rahu and Ketu move in backward direction only and Jupiter, Venus, Mars, Mercury and Saturn move in forward as well as in backward direction. This dual movement of these five planets among navagraha is what has made some astrologers and researchers devote many years of their lives in order to find the true meaning of such concept of retrograde motion of these five planets which generally move in forward direction.

Hence different astrologers have assigned different meanings to such retrograde planets where some of them believe that if a planet goes retrograde in a horoscope, it starts working negatively in that horoscope. The reason assigned to such negativity is the fact that since such planet has started moving backward instead of moving forward, it has become negative as moving back is considered as a negative practice. Some other astrologers believe that if a planet goes retrograde in a horoscope, it reverses its general nature, which means that if this planet is otherwise supposed to work positively in that horoscope, it will start working negatively and if this planet is otherwise supposed to work negatively in that horoscope, it will start working positively when it goes retrograde. The logic assigned to this belief is that the movement in opposite direction indicates the movement of working nature in opposite direction too.

Yet some other astrologers believe that if a planet goes retrograde in its sign of exaltation, it will work negatively in the horoscope whereas if a planet goes retrograde in its sign of debilitation, it will work positively in the horoscope. Finally there are some other astrologers who believe that the concept of change in direction of movement of these planets has got nothing to do with their working nature and accordingly, retrograde planets behave just like the forward moving planets and nothing else. These different theories and beliefs related to the working nature of retrograde planets have caused a situation of much confusion in the mind of an average person interested in astrology as he gets confused, which one of these theories he should believe and which one he should not.

With the grace of Lord Shiva, I have myself spent a good number of years researching in the concept of retrograde planets and in finding the true meaning behind such concept of their retrogradation. It always intrigued me why a planet which generally moves forward starts moving backward? Why do Sun and Moon only move in forward direction, Rahu and Ketu only move in backward direction whereas Jupiter, Venus, Mars, Mercury and Saturn move in forward as well as in backward direction? There must be some meaning to it as otherwise there is no sense in the fact that only five specific planets among navagraha possess the ability to move in both direction whereas the other four planets can move in one direction only.

So what is the meaning of these planets being blessed with the ability to move in forward as well as in backward direction and what could change in a horoscope when a generally forward moving planet changes its direction and starts moving in backward direction? The answer to all these questions is that there is definitely something different happening when a forward moving planet suddenly starts moving in backward direction. Accordingly its behavior in a horoscope changes, sometimes by a small margin; sometimes considerably and sometimes it may start behaving in the exactly opposite manner. Through the coming lines, we will get to know some surprising, important as well as valuable facts related to the behavior of retrograde planets in a horoscope.

When a planet goes retrograde in a horoscope, it may change its working nature in that horoscope where the percentage of change in such working nature depends on the planet which has gone retrograde, the house of placement of such retrograde planet as well as the sign of placement of such retrograde planet in a horoscope and on the overall tone of the horoscope of in question. For example, if retrograde Jupiter is placed in the ninth house of a horoscope in the sign of Cancer, it may only change slightly in nature and there also, only a part of its behavior may change. On the other hand, if retrograde Jupiter is placed in the fifth house of horoscope in the sign of Cancer, it may indicate much more change in its behavior compared to the first case, though it may still remain on the same line of positivity or negativity as otherwise indicated by the overall horoscope.

However if the same retrograde Jupiter is placed in the first house of a horoscope in the sign of Cancer, it can even reverse its working nature in the horoscope, which means that it may start behaving negatively in such a horoscope if it is otherwise meant to work positively in the horoscope and it may start working positively in that horoscope if it is otherwise meant to work negatively in that horoscope. Similarly, retrograde Jupiter placed in the first house of horoscope in the sign of Libra may not indicate much change in its behavior whereas retrograde Jupiter placed in the eighth house of a horoscope in the sign of Libra may change its behavior to considerable extent. Therefore, the study of retrograde planets in astrology is very deep as well as very subjective.

One interesting fact related to these five planets which can move in forward as well as in backward direction is that once they start moving backward which means once they go retrograde, they become somewhat moody and accordingly they may start overdoing certain jobs assigned to them or they may not even do what is expected of them. Technically speaking, a retrograde planet can sometimes gain extra strength by virtue of being retrograde and it can sometimes gain extra weakness by virtue of being retrograde, depending on the overall tone of the horoscope. But one thing is common in both these cases, which is the fact that retrograde planets need more attention as their behavior is not like the other planets which move in one direction only.

In the coming series of articles, I am going to explain some of the commonly occurring results when each one of these five planets goes retrograde when placed in different houses of a horoscope.

Retrograde Jupiter in 1st House

When showing retrograde in a horoscope, Jupiter can cause various types of positive or negative results for the native depending on its working nature, strength, level of activity and some other factors. The natives having retrograde Jupiter in their horoscopes may experience some of the below mentioned results depending on the placement of retrograde Jupiter in various houses of their horoscopes. The scope of a planet to cause various effects in any house of a horoscope is vast and it can't be contained in some words but I'll still mention some commonly occurring positive and negative effects of Jupiter when retrograde and placed in various houses of a horoscope.

Retrograde Jupiter in 1st House: First house is undoubtedly the most important house of a horoscope as it can affect almost any sphere of a native's life either positively or negatively due to which, the placement of any positive as well as negative planet in this house of the horoscope demands utmost attention as the planetary influences registered in the first house of a horoscope are in decisive position when it comes to render good or bad things to the native having such influences, in most cases. When working positively, retrograde Jupiter placed in the first house of a horoscope can bless the native with good, very good or great amount of luck depending on the type and strength of this placement as well as depending on the overall tone of the horoscope of the native in question.

This luck factor rendered by Jupiter stands for the fruit of good karmas done by the native, in the domain of Jupiter and since the domain of Jupiter is a very big domain, accordingly it can bring great amount of luck to the native under its benefic influence if such native has done considerable amount of good karmas in his past lives, especially in his recent past life. Benefic retrograde Jupiter in first house of a horoscope can bless the native with professional success, good marriage, finances, fame, recognition, good health, long life, good children, wisdom, spiritual progress and many other good things as the scope of the good thing that this planet can render to a native when benefic in nature, is very wide and hence it can bless the native with good results in almost any sphere of his life.

Benefic retrograde Jupiter in first house of a horoscope can render professional success to the native and accordingly many natives blessed by this placement may achieve success in different professional spheres depending on the type and strength of this placement as well as depending on their overall horoscopes. Such benefic placement is especially very good at creating special abilities in the native related to the fields of spiritualism, religion, overall wisdom, teaching, preaching, service for humanity, paranormal, supernatural and other divine sciences, and many other such similar fields. Accordingly some natives under this benefic influence may have special abilities as well as strong inclinations towards one of these fields or even more than one of these fields. If this benefic influence is strong and the overall horoscope is supportive, the native under this influence may actively follow one of these spheres as his profession or as a full time job.

For example, the presence of benefic retrograde Jupiter in first house of a horoscope in the sign of Pisces can create good, very good or great amount of spiritual, religious or some of the other already mentioned tendencies in the native and accordingly, the native may have an interest in following one of these lines as his field of profession. Hence this native may choose one of these professions depending on the other factors in his horoscope. Looking at these different possibilities, the presence of benefic Venus or Rahu in the sixth house of the same horoscope in the sign of Leo can bend the native towards being an astrologer or other such types of professionals who practice in all types of faiths related to these categories.

The combined effect of these benefic influences can also make the native pursue his higher studies in the field of medical science and such native may especially be interested in the branch of medical which deals with the issues related to women or which deals with the issues related to the heart. It means that if such native follows medical profession under the combined effect of these benefic influences, he is more likely to become a gynecologist or a psychiatrist. However if benefic Rahu, benefic Mars or benefic Sun is placed in the eighth house of the same horoscope, the native under the combined effect of these beneficiary influences is more likely to follow the path of astrology or some other such faiths and accordingly, he may become a professional astrologer or any other such type of professional dealing in one of these faiths.

If benefic Moon is placed in the fourth house of the same horoscope in the sign of Gemini, the native much achieve very good amount of success and fame as an astrologer as the combined effect of these benefic influences can further enhance the professional scope of the native. If benefic Mercury is present in the tenth house of the same horoscope in the sign of Sagittarius, the native under the combined effect of these benefic influences may achieve very good or even great amount of success through his profession in astrology or in one of other such faiths. Such native may become famous on national level and he may have a big number of people following him.

Some natives under this benefic influence may also have creative interests and accordingly they may rise in various creative fields and they may achieve success on different levels depending on the type and strength of this placement as well as depending on the overall tone of their horoscopes. Some natives under such benefic influence can become professional song writers, singers, actors, directors and many other types of professionals dealing in creative fields and they may achieve good amount of success and fame through such professional fields if their overall horoscopes are favorable. For example, the presence of benefic retrograde Jupiter in the first house of a horoscope in the sign of Leo can make the native interested in acting, directing or writing and accordingly such native may pursue one of these fields depending on the other factors in his horoscope.

For instance, the presence of benefic Venus in the tenth house of the same horoscope in the sign of Taurus can bend the native more towards acting or singing and accordingly the native may become a singer or actor, under the combined effect of these benefic planets. If benefic Mercury or benefic Rahu is present in the second house of the same horoscope in the sign of Virgo, the native may be more inclined towards being a singer and accordingly he may choose his primary field of profession as singing, though he may work as an actor also, due to the combined effect of benefic retrograde Jupiter in the first house and benefic Venus in the tenth house of his horoscope.

However if benefic Mercury is placed in fifth house of the same horoscope in the sign of Sagittarius and benefic Rahu is either placed in the tenth house of the horoscope in the sign of Taurus or it is placed in fifth house of the same horoscope in the sign of Sagittarius, the native under the combined effect of these benefic influences will be bent more towards acting than singing. Accordingly, the native may become a movie actor and he may achieve good amount of success and fame through this profession though he may still sing in some of his movies, due to the combined effect of benefic planets which promote singing abilities in him.

However, if a combination of benefic Mercury and benefic Sun is present in the fifth house of the same horoscope when benefic Venus and benefic Rahu are placed in the tenth house of this horoscope and benefic retrograde Jupiter is placed in the first house of this horoscope, the native under the combined effect of these benefic influences may achieve success on a very big level and accordingly, he may become a well recognized, successful and famous movie star. Apart from this, benefic retrograde Jupiter in the first house of a horoscope can bless the native with success in many types of professions depending on the type and strength of this placement as well as depending on the overall tone of the horoscope of the native under consideration.

Benefic retrograde Jupiter in the first house of a horoscope can also render good or very good results related to marriage and married life of the native and accordingly, the native benefitting from this positive influence may witness different types and different quantum of good results through their marriages, depending on their overall horoscopes. For example, the presence of benefic retrograde Jupiter in first house of a horoscope in the sign of Aries can get the native married at a proper age and such native may also get a life partner who is strong by character and who provides much strength to the native after marriage. Such partner is likely to motivate the native to do better things, perform better and achieve more and more in life due to which, the native blessed and motivated by such life partner may achieve much more in his life after his marriage, compared to his achievements before his marriage.

Such life partner is not only likely to motivate and advise the native from time to time, he or she is also likely to stand by the native through all thick and thin, thereby supporting him in all his major decisions. If benefic Venus is also present in the first house of the same horoscope in the sign of Aries, the native under the combined influence of these benefic planets may get a very strong, capable and supportive life partner, say wife for example, and such wife may also be very good at the skill of socializing and connecting with more and more people. The native blessed by and supported by such wife may start achieving more and more success after his marriage and such wife may be so good at socializing that she may become more recognized and connected in the personal circle of the native, with the passage of time. It means that such wife may have a better equation with many of native's friends and relatives, than the native himself has.

In addition to this, benefic retrograde Jupiter in the first house of a horoscope can bless the native with many other types of good results through marriage and many other spheres of his life, depending on the type and strength of such benefic retrograde Jupiter in first house of his horoscope as well as depending on the overall tone of the horoscope of the native. On the other hand, retrograde Jupiter placed in the first house of a horoscope can do damage in many spheres of a native's life, if it turns negative and accordingly many native's suffering from this malefic influence may witness bad results in many spheres of their lives depending on important factors in their horoscopes.

Malefic retrograde Jupiter in first house of a horoscope can cause serious problems in marriage and married life of the native and accordingly some natives under the effect of this bad influence may have to face many problems related to their marriages. Some of these natives may not get married at proper times and they may have to wait till long or very long in order to get married whereas some other natives suffering from this malefic influence may have to face many problems through their marriages. For example, the presence of malefic retrograde Jupiter in the first house of a horoscope in the sign of Aries can delay as well as disturb the marriage of the native where the amount of delay and disturbance depends on the other important factors in the horoscope of the native.

Looking at some of these factors, if malefic Mars, malefic Rahu or malefic Saturn is also placed in the first house of the same horoscope in the sign of Aries, the native under the combined effect of these malefic influences may have to wait till late or very late in his life, in order to get married and he may also have to face many problems after his marriage. Among these combinations, the combination of malefic retrograde Jupiter and malefic Mars in the first house of a horoscope in the sign of Aries can easily break one marriage of the native after making him suffer many problems through it. The possibility of a bad and broken marriage further increases if such malefic Mars forms Manglik Dosh in the first house of the horoscope and accordingly, the native under the combined effect of these two malefic influences may have to face a divorce after facing many problems in his marriage.

The presence of malefic Rahu with malefic retrograde Jupiter in the first house of horoscope in the sign of Aries can cause even more damage and the combination of these malefic influences can also easily break one marriage of the native. This combination can become even more troublesome if malefic Rahu placed in first house of the horoscope forms Anant Kaal Sarp Dosh in the horoscope, along with the participation of Ketu placed in the seventh house of the same horoscope in the sign of Libra. If this happens, the native under the combined effect of these malefic influences may have to witness more than one divorce after facing very bad marriages, unless there are some marriage saving combinations present in his horoscope.

Talking about such marriage saving combinations, the presence of benefic Venus in the seventh house of the same horoscope in the sign of Libra along with malefic Ketu can still try and save the first marriage of the native and it can almost certainly save the second marriage, provided the overall horoscope is supportive for the second marriage. If benefic Moon also joins benefic Venus in seventh house of the same horoscope, the presence of this combination of benefic Moon and benefic Venus in the seventh house of this horoscope in the sign of Libra along with malefic Ketu can save even the first marriage of the native after some initial disturbances.

The native under the combined malefic influence of malefic retrograde Jupiter and malefic Rahu in the first house of his horoscope and malefic Ketu in the seventh house of his horoscope may have to face many problems in his first marriage due to these malefic influences but the positive effect of benefic combination of Venus and Moon in the seventh house of his horoscope can still save this marriage. Such native may have to face problems in the early years of his marriage due to the effect of malefic retrograde Jupiter and other malefic planets but he may witness a very good and strong marriage after surviving through these initial bad years.

Malefic retrograde Jupiter in the first house of a horoscope can also trouble the native on account of problems related to his profession, health, reputation, longevity and many other spheres of his life and accordingly many natives suffering from this malefic influence may have to witness problems in some of these spheres depending on the type and strength of such malefic retrograde Jupiter in their horoscopes, as well as depending on the overall tone of their horoscopes.

Retrograde Jupiter in 2nd House

When working positively, retrograde Jupiter placed in second house of a horoscope can bless the native with good, very good or great results related to the fields of marriage, profession, children, health, wealth, fame and many other spheres of his life, where the type of results as well as the quantum of results received by different natives under this benefic influence vary from native to native, depending on the type and strength of this placement as well as depending on the overall tone of the horoscopes of different natives.

Benefic retrograde Jupiter placed in second house of a horoscope can bless the native with success in a wide variety of professional spheres and accordingly the natives under this influence may achieve success through many types of professional spheres. Some natives under this benefic influence may become interested in running some type of business or practice instead of working for other people and accordingly these natives may engage in different types of businesses or practices based on their overall horoscopes. For example, the presence of benefic retrograde Jupiter in the sign of Capricorn can make the native run his own business and such native may start from a shop or a showroom which deals with a variety of products required by different people. However, this placement on its own can't guarantee much success through such business as Jupiter is debilitated in the sign of Capricorn and accordingly it can't deliver much due to its physical weakness and it needs support from other positive planets in the horoscope.

If benefic Saturn is also placed in the second house of the same horoscope in the sign of Capricorn, such benefic Saturn can not only provide much strength to the debilitated Jupiter as Saturn is the Lord of Capricorn, but a combination of these two benefic planets can also improve the overall results achieved by such native, to a very good extent. As a result, the native under the combined influence of these two benefic planets may now start with a reasonable looking shop or showroom, but over a few years, he may expand his showroom many times and he may start earning very good incomes through his business. Such a benefic combination of these two planets generally promises a very good growth which is usually slow to start with but which is very steady once achieved, provided the overall horoscope of the native allows it.

The presence of benefic Mercury in the second house of the same horoscope in the sign of Capricorn, along with benefic retrograde Jupiter and benefic Saturn in the same house can further enhance the good results received by the native and accordingly, the native under the combined influence of these three benefic planets may now witness success on a much bigger level. Such native may start from a small shop or showroom though, but he is likely to achieve success at a fast pace and within a matter of years, he is likely to be the owner of more than one big showroom, shopping mall or a chain of showrooms or shopping malls. Such native is likely to earn very good amount of money through such showrooms or shopping malls and he is likely to achieve more and more incomes as well as build more business establishments, year after year, provided his overall horoscope allows it.

Benefic retrograde Jupiter in the second house of a horoscope can also bless the native with creative abilities and accordingly some natives benefitting from this placement may achieve success through some creative or artistic field where the type of field chosen by different natives and the amount of success achieved by them varies depending on their overall horoscopes. For example, the presence of benefic retrograde Jupiter in the second house of a horoscope in the sign of Libra can render good singing abilities to the native and accordingly such native may become interested in being a professional singer, though this placement alone may not make him a professional singer and it may need support from other factors in his horoscope.

Looking at these other factors, if benefic Venus is also present in the second house of the same horoscope in the sign of Libra, the native under the combined effect of these two benefic planets may actually become a professional singer and he may achieve good amount of success through his profession. The native under the combined effect of benefic retrograde Jupiter and benefic Venus in the second house of his horoscope in the sign of Libra is likely to have a sweet and soothing voice and he is likely to be a singer who achieve more fame and recognition through the genre of love songs or party songs, though he may sing songs related to various other genres also.

If benefic Moon also joins this combination in the second house of the same horoscope, the combined effect of benefic retrograde Jupiter, benefic Venus and benefic Moon in the second house of the horoscope in the sign of Libra can render great amount of success to the native, through the profession of singing. Accordingly, such native may become a popular singer and he may deliver many hit songs which fetch him very good amount of incomes and fame, for a long period of time. If a combination of benefic Mercury and benefic Sun is present in the tenth house of the same horoscope in the sing of Gemini, the native under the combined influence of these five benefic planets may do extraordinarily at his profession and he may achieve phenomenal amount of success as a singer.

Such native may not only become one of the lead singers of his country but he may also get fame and recognition in some foreign countries also, as the combined effect of these benefic planets is very well capable of blessing the native with fame and recognition in foreign countries also. The native under the combined effect of such benefic influences can also receive more than one formal award on national level, for some of his songs. If benefic Rahu is present in the second house of the same horoscope in the sign of Libra, it can further enhance the positive equation and the native under the combined effect of these benefic planets may not only achieve success in his country, he may also start singing in some foreign language and he may achieve good amount of success and recognition in foreign countries also. Such native may also receive an award of the highest order on international level, for his singing, provided there are no other restricting combinations or placements in his horoscope.

The presence of benefic retrograde Jupiter in the second house of a horoscope can also bless the native with good results through his marriage and accordingly some natives benefitting from this positive influence may witness different types and quantum of good results depending on the type and strength of this placement as well as depending on their overall horoscopes. Some natives under this benefic influences may get married to beautiful, well mannered and civilized life partners who can not only enrich their marriages through their beauty as well as qualities but who can also provide much support and strength to such natives, by virtue of many of their qualities as well as by virtue of their support for these natives.

For example, the presence of benefic retrograde Jupiter in the second house of the horoscope of a male in the sign of Taurus can get him married to a girl who is beautiful, well mannered and who is very much devoted to the overall concept of marriage. It means that such female believes in making her marriage work and she puts in her best effort to improve the quality of her marriage, play her due part in the marriage and support her husband at each and every front of his life. The native receives many pleasures through his marriage and he also receives good amount of support, motivation and advice from his wife from time to time due to which he enjoys a good marriage and his overall success and status also starts rising after marriage.

If benefic Venus or benefic Moon is also present in the second house of the same horoscope in the sign of Taurus, the native under the combined effect of benefic retrograde Jupiter and benefic Moon or benefic Venus can witness even better results in the field of his marriage. Such a native may get a wife from a rich family or a professionally well established wife who may not only enrich his life with all the already mentioned good things, but who may also bring in good amount of money or financial support through her family or through her profession. As a result, the financial equation of the native under the combined effect of these benefic influences may improve a lot after his marriage and he may witness much better quality of life after his marriage.

On the other hand, the presence of retrograde Jupiter in the second house of a horoscope can cause problems in many spheres of a native's life if it turns negative. Accordingly, many natives under the effect of such malefic influence may have to face problems in many spheres of their lives including marriage and profession, where the type and intensity of these problems may vary from native to native depending on the type and strength of this malefic influence as well as depending on the overall tone of the horoscopes of different natives in consideration.

Malefic retrograde Jupiter in second house of a horoscope can cause problems in the professional sphere of the native and accordingly some natives under the effect of this malefic influence may have to face different types of problems related to their professional spheres. Some natives under this bad influence may not be able to establish themselves professionally till late or very late in their lives and they may have to keep changing their jobs from time to time till late or very late in their lives. If such malefic influence is strong and it is supported by some other malefic planets in the horoscope, the native under the combined effect of such malefic influences may have to remain jobless or without profession, many times in his life or for a continuous period of many years in his life.

For example, the presence of malefic retrograde Jupiter in the second house of a horoscope in the sign of Gemini can cause problems related to the professional sphere of the native and accordingly the native under this malefic influence may not be able to establish himself well in his profession. Such native may have to work for low paying jobs though he may have good academic qualifications as such malefic influence can prove very bad for the income and overall financial aspect of the native. If malefic Ketu or malefic Mars is also present in the second house of the same horoscope in the sign of Gemini, the combined effect of these malefic influences can further intensify the problems.

Accordingly the native under the combined effect of these malefic influences may have to face serious financial problems up to 42 years of his life or throughout his life and he may also have to remain jobless for many years of his life, provided there are no saving factors in his horoscope. For example, the presence of benefic Mercury or benefic Saturn in the tenth house of the same horoscope in the sign of Aquarius can still ensure that the native secures profession on permanent basis. It means that though the combined effect of malefic retrograde Jupiter and malefic Ketu or malefic Mars in the second house of his horoscope can make him work for low paying jobs and it can also make him lose his job many times in his life, the benefic effect of positive Mercury or benefic Saturn ensures that the native still earns decent amount of money through his profession and he keeps getting new jobs quickly, as and when he loses his jobs.

Malefic retrograde Jupiter in second house of a horoscope can also cause problems related to the marriage aspect of the native and accordingly some natives under this malefic influence may have to face different types of problems related to their marriages. Some of these natives may have to wait till late or very late in their lives in order to get married whereas some other natives may have to suffer a lot through their marriages and they may also have to face one or more than one broken marriage. For example, the presence of malefic retrograde Jupiter in the second house of a horoscope in the sign of Scorpio can delay the marriage of the native for a long or very long period of time and the same malefic placement is also fully capable of breaking the marriage of the native after causing many problems in such marriage.

Hence such native may get married late or vary late in his life and this problem can become even worse if such malefic retrograde Jupiter is present in the second house in the horoscope of a female in the sign of Scorpio. The female under such malefic influence may have to wait for a long period of time in order to get married and if such malefic influence is supported by some other malefic planets, her problems may intensify even more. For example, if malefic Venus is also present in the second house of the same horoscope in the sign of Scorpio, the combined effect of these malefic influences can cause long delay in her marriage and she may get married after 35 years of her age, unless there are some marriage favoring combinations in her horoscope.

Talking about these combinations, the presence of a benefic Chandra Mangal Yoga in the seventh house of the same horoscope in the sign of Aries can still get such female native married with some delay, despite the combined malefic effect of retrograde Jupiter and malefic Venus in the second house of her horoscope. Such Chandra Mangal Yoga formed by the combination of benefic Moon and benefic Mars in the seventh house of this horoscope can get this female native married around 28 or 29 years of her life and she may even get married around 23rd or 24th year of her life, if benefic Mars present in the seventh house of this horoscope in the sign of Aries forms Manglik Yoga in the horoscope, apart from forming benefic Chandra Mangal Yoga with benefic Moon in the seventh house. The combined effect of such benefic Chandra Mangal Yoga and Manglik Yoga can reduce the malefic effect of negative combination of malefic retrograde Jupiter and malefic Venus in the second house of the same horoscope in the sign of Scorpio to great extent, and such native may not only get married at a proper age, but she may also witness a good marriage after facing some problems in the early years of her marriage.

Retrograde Jupiter in 3rd House

Benefic retrograde Jupiter placed in third house of a horoscope can bless the native with good results in profession, marriage, finances, overall health and many other things. Accordingly, many natives under the effect of this benefic influence may witness good results in different spheres of their lives where the type of these results and quantum of these result can be different for different natives depending on the type and strength of this placement, as well as depending on the overall tone of horoscopes of these different natives.

Benefic retrograde Jupiter in third house of a horoscope can render success to the native through a wide variety of professions and accordingly, different natives may succeed in different professional spheres, by virtue of this benefic influence. Some natives under this benefic influence may start their own business or practice instead of working for someone else, as this benefic influence is good at blessing the native with success through business or some type of practice, though it is equally capable of blessing the native with success in some job. The type of business or practice chosen by different natives under this benefic influence may be different depending on the overall tone of the horoscopes of these natives.

For example, the presence of benefic retrograde Jupiter in the third house of a horoscope in the sign of Aquarius can make the native start a business related to telecommunication, networking, computers or some other such type of business related to some type of communication or networking. As a result, the native may either run a small shop dealing in one of these solutions or he may become the owner of a big company providing one of these solutions, depending on the other important factors in his horoscope. This placement alone is not capable of blessing the native with very good amount of success and accordingly the native may just be the owner of a small shop or showroom dealing in items related to telecommunications, computers or networking, if there are no other supporting factors in the horoscope of such native.

However, the presence of benefic Mercury in the third house of the same horoscope can change this equation and the combined effect of such benefic Mercury and benefic retrograde Jupiter in the third house of this horoscope in the sign of Aquarius can bless the native with much more success. Accordingly the native may own a big showroom dealing in one of the fields mentioned in this example and he may also have a franchise for some famous company which provides networking, telecommunication, internet or other such type of solutions. Such native may earn good amount of money through such channels and he may keep achieving success year after year, though this combination alone may not promise success on a very high level, and it needs more support.

Talking about such support, if benefic Venus or benefic Rahu is placed in the seventh house of the same horoscope in the sign of Gemini while a combination of benefic retrograde Jupiter and benefic Mercury is present in the third house of the same horoscope in the sign of Aquarius, the native under the combined benefic influence of these planets may achieve very good amount of success through business related to one of these fields and he may experience growth at a fast pace. Such native may have exclusive franchise of one or more than one service providers in his region and he may make very good amount of money through such franchise.

If benefic Moon is placed in the tenth house of this horoscope in the sign of Virgo, the amount of success achieved by the native under the combined effect these benefic influences may increase many times and such native may even start his own company which provides one of these solutions to the clients, on a state or even on a national level. For example, the native under the effect of these benefic influences may start a telephone services providing company on a state level and he may earn very good amount of money and recognition through it. If the overall horoscope of such native is supportive, he may even witness his company growing on a national level, like the placement of benefic Sun in the second house of this horoscope, in the sign of Capricorn can render even bigger amount of professional success to the native under the combined effect of these benefic influences.

Benefic retrograde Jupiter in third house of a horoscope can also render creative abilities to the native and accordingly some natives benefitting from this influence may become interested in writing, acting, direction or in some other type of creative field like photography or video making. If there are other supporting influences present in the horoscope of this native, he may become a professional dealing in one of these fields and he may achieve success and fame through one of such professional fields. For example, the presence of benefic retrograde Jupiter in the third house of a horoscope in the sign of Gemini can bless the native with good writing abilities and accordingly such native may make a career choice in a field which honors his writing skills. Such native may become a newspaper reporter, magazine reporter, song writer, script writer or even a book or novel writer depending on the other important factors present in his horoscope.

Taking a look at a few possible combinations, the presence of benefic Mercury in the third house of this horoscope in the sign of Gemini can bend the native more towards writing for news papers or for the magazines dealing with the coverage of crime and criminal activities. The presence of benefic Mars in the third house of this horoscope in the sign of Gemini can further enhance this equation and the native under the combined effect of such benefic retrograde Jupiter, Mercury and Mars may become a well established news paper reporter, especially a crime reporter. If benefic Rahu or benefic Moon is present in the second house of the same horoscope in the sign of Taurus, the native under the combined effect of these benefic planets may start his career as a news paper reporter but he may eventually start working for some electronic news channel. Here also, this native works as a crime reporter or a specialist reporter on politics, and he may achieve very good amount of success and fame as this type of reporter.

However if benefic retrograde Jupiter is placed in the third house of a horoscope in the sign of Gemini and benefic Saturn is placed in the same house instead of benefic Mercury, the native under the combined influence of such benefic Jupiter and Saturn may become a professional writer who writes scripts for movies, television programs or who writes articles on various other topics. Such native may work for some magazine or he may have his own blog through which he may write on topics which provide tips for improvement in various spheres of life. If benefic Sun is present in the ninth house of the same horoscope in the sign of Sagittarius, the native may become an even bigger writer and instead of writing small pieces of work, he may start writing books on various topics. Such native may achieve good amount of success and fame through his books and he may also have a healthy amount of fan base, which likes his style of writing.

If benefic Rahu, benefic Venus or benefic Moon is placed in the tenth house of the same horoscope in the sign of Capricorn, the success achieved by the native under such benefic influences may increase further and accordingly the native may become a famous book writer. Such native may not only be able to attract readers from his own country, but his style of writing as well as his concepts may attract a good amount of foreign readers also. This can be especially true if a combination of benefic Venus and benefic Rahu is present in the tenth house of the same horoscope in the sign of Capricorn, as the combined effect of these two benefic planets further combined with benefic Sun in the ninth house, benefic retrograde Jupiter and benefic Saturn in the third house of this horoscope can render phenomenal success on international level, to the native under its influence. Such native may not only achieve fame and success on international level, but he may also receive formal awards for some of his books.

Some natives under the benefic influence of retrograde Jupiter in third house of their horoscopes can also make a career choice in some type of coaching, consulting, guiding or marketing field and they may achieve different levels of success in one of such fields, depending on the type and strength of such placement as well as depending on their overall horoscopes. For example, the presence of benefic retrograde Jupiter in the third house of a horoscope in the sign of Capricorn can make bless the native with the abilities to be a good teacher and especially a good coach on some topic and accordingly this native may make a career choice in some type of coaching like he may provide professional coaching for some competitive exams or for some other subjects.

Since Jupiter is debilitated in the sign of Capricorn, this placement of benefic retrograde Jupiter in the third house of a horoscope alone can't promise much success to the native, in most cases, and this benefic influence needs to be supported by some other positive influence. Otherwise, the native may keep working for a coaching institute for a big part of his life, for an average salary and with an average amount of recognition as a coach or as a teacher. However, if benefic Saturn, benefic Mars or benefic Rahu is also present in the third house of this horoscope in the sign of Capricorn, the native under the combined effect of these benefic influences may achieve much more success as a coach and he may also start running his own coaching center. Such native may earn good amount of money and recognition through such coaching center, though the combination of these two benefic planets in the third house of his horoscope alone can't promise incomes beyond a certain level, and more positive influences are required in order to see more success.

If benefic retrograde Jupiter is present in the third house of a horoscope in the sign of Capricorn along with benefic Mars and benefic Moon is placed either in the fourth house of this horoscope in the sign of Aquarius, or in the tenth house of the same horoscope in the sign of Leo, the native under the combined effect of these benefic influence may achieve even more success through his coaching business and he may own more than one coaching centers in more than one cities. If such benefic Moon is placed in the tenth house of this horoscope while a combination of benefic retrograde Jupiter and benefic Mars is placed in the third house of this horoscope, the presence of benefic Venus or benefic Saturn in the tenth house of this horoscope can further enhance the results achieved by the native. Accordingly, the native under the combined effect of all these benefic influence may own a chain of coaching centers which operates throughout a state, many states or throughout the country, provided the overall horoscope of the native allows all this.

On the other hand, malefic retrograde Jupiter placed in third house of a horoscope can cause many problems related to marriage, profession, health and many other spheres of a native's life and accordingly, many natives suffering from this malefic influence may have to face bad results in different spheres of their lives depending on the type and strength of this placement as well as depending on their overall horoscopes. Malefic retrograde Jupiter can cause problems in the professional sphere of the native under its influence due to which many natives suffering from this bad influence may face one type of problem or the other in their professional sphere.

Some natives under this malefic influence may have to suffer on account of delayed as well as below average professional success, which means that they may not get professionally established at proper ages and they may have to struggle till late or very late in their lives, in order to achieve professional stability. It also means that some of these natives may further have to face many problems in their professional spheres even when they are able to get stable professions. For example, the presence of malefic retrograde Jupiter in the third house of a horoscope in the sign of Cancer can cause delays, disturbances and losses related to the professional sphere of the native.

It should be noted that though Jupiter is exalted in Cancer and some astrologers believe that an exalted planet always works positively in the horoscope, it is not the case as the placement of a planet in different signs including its sign of exaltation and its sign of debilitation is just a measure of its physical strength, and it is not a measure of its working nature in a horoscope. Such malefic retrograde Jupiter placed in the third house of a horoscope in its sign of exaltation which means in Cancer, can cause serious amount of damage not only in the professional sphere of the native, but also in marriage and health aspect of the native. Hence the natives under such malefic influence may feel the heat of such negative exalted Jupiter in many spheres of their lives, where most such natives suffer the most in the field of their profession, by virtue of such malefic influence.

The presence of malefic or even benefic Saturn in the twelfth house of the same horoscope in the sign of Aries can make the situation even worse as the placement of Saturn in its sign of debilitation can result in inability of Saturn to protect its specific significances which means that Saturn may not be fully able to deliver the results related to ninth as well as tenth house of this horoscope, where the two signs ruled by Saturn, which are Capricorn and Aquarius, fall respectively. Hence the combined effect of such malefic retrograde Jupiter in the third house of this horoscope in the sign of Cancer, and debilitated Saturn in the twelfth house of the same horoscope can make the native suffer a lot on professional front. If Malefic Ketu or malefic Mars is also present in the twelfth house of the same horoscope, in the sign of Aries, the combined effect of these malefic influences can make the native remain jobless for a long part of his life and if there are some other malefic influences present in the horoscope, the native may have to spend almost his entire life, without any significant profession.

Malefic retrograde Jupiter in third house of a horoscope can also trouble the native with issues related to his health and accordingly some natives under such malefic influence may suffer from various health related issues and diseases where the type and intensity of these diseases depend on the type and strength of this malefic influence, as well as on the overall tone of the horoscopes of these natives. For example, the presence of malefic retrograde Jupiter in the third house of a horoscope in the sign of Aquarius can trouble the native on account of many health problems from time to time and the native may even suffer from a permanent type of disease.

If malefic Venus, malefic Saturn, Malefic Ketu or Malefic Rahu is also present in the third house of the same horoscope, the native may suffer from a serious and permanent type of disease or a long lasting disease and he may have to suffer a lot on account of such diseases. In extreme cases of this type, the native may get afflicted with some life threatening disease which may trouble the native for many years and which may eventually claim his life. For example, the presence of malefic retrograde Jupiter in the third house of a horoscope in the sign of Aquarius along with malefic Ketu and malefic Moon or Mars can afflict the native with a life threatening disease and such native may die at a relatively young or very young age, by virtue of this disease.

Retrograde Jupiter in 4th House

When working positively, retrograde Jupiter placed in fourth house of a horoscope can bless the native with good results in marriage, profession, health, education, lifespan, spiritualism and many other spheres of his life. Accordingly, many natives benefitting from this placement may witness different type and different quantum of results depending on the type and strength of this placement, as well as depending on the overall tone of horoscopes of these natives.

The presence of benefic retrograde Jupiter in fourth house of a horoscope can prove to be a very good placement as far as the marriage aspect of the native is concerned and accordingly some natives benefitting from this placement may see good, very good or great results through their marriages. Some natives under this benefic influence may get married at proper ages and they also get life partners who are very caring, who invest good amount of time in their marriages and who bring good value to the lives of these natives. For example, the presence of benefic retrograde Jupiter in the fourth house of the horoscope of a male native in the sign of Sagittarius can bless him with a wife who is well educated, well cultured and who believes a lot in the concept of marriage.

Such wife may take very good care of native's day to day needs and she may also be an expert when it comes to beautify the residential house of the native and in fact, she may be very good at beautifying the overall marriage of the native. The house of such native is generally upgraded to more beautiful, cleaner and more attractive level after the marriage, where everything seems to be placed on its proper place, in a neat and clean way. If benefic Moon is also placed in the fourth house of this horoscope along with benefic retrograde Jupiter in the sign of Sagittarius, the native under the combined effect of these benefic planets may not only get married to a caring and good wife, but the overall fortune of this native may also see a good rise after his marriage and he may keep making more and more progress in his profession, after his marriage.

This native is also likely to get good amount of support from his wife as she may motivate and advise her from time to time, in relation to his profession as well as in relation to many other things and such advice may work well for the native, in most cases. The presence of benefic Venus in the fourth house of the same horoscope in the sign of Sagittarius can further enhance the benefits received by the native through his marriage and accordingly the native under the combined effect of benefic retrograde Jupiter, benefic Moon and benefic Venus in the fourth house of his horoscope in the sign of Sagittarius may witness even better results through his marriage. The native under the combined effect of these benefic influences may get married to a very beautiful and charming wife who may not only be good at the art of beautifying the house and marriage of the native, but who may possess many other good qualities too.

She may be a very good cook and accordingly she may take very good care of the native's taste in different foods. Such wife may also be very social and she may welcome each and every one of native's relatives and acquaintances with open heart due to which the native may witness that many of his old as well as new relationships have become much stronger, after his wife has come to his life. This is due to the fact that his wife takes such good care of people who are important in his life that these people get more closely attached to the native, they start caring more for the native and they start doing more for the native, largely due to the good things done by his wife to them. This is the type of wife who may become more popular and more respected even in native's personal circle, only within a few years of his marriage, by virtue of her good deeds.

Some natives under the benefic influence of retrograde Jupiter in the fourth house of their horoscopes may get married to very rich and established partners whereas some of these natives may get married to someone hailing from a foreign country and they may get settled in that foreign country, by virtue of such marriage. For example, the presence of benefic retrograde Jupiter in the fourth house of a horoscope in the sign of Cancer can bless the native with a life partner hailing from a foreign country and accordingly such native may get married to a foreigner or to a person who originally belongs to his own country but who is now a citizen of a foreign country. If benefic Rahu is also placed in the fourth house the same horoscope in the sign of Cancer or if benefic Venus is placed in the ninth or twelfth house of this horoscope, such native may get settled in a foreign country, by virtue of his marriage to a person hailing from a that country.

Taking a look at another possibility, the presence of benefic retrograde Jupiter in the fourth house of a horoscope in the sign of Aquarius can get the native married to rich or established person and accordingly the native under the effect of this influence may get married to someone rich or someone who holds a position of power and authority in some government or private organization. If benefic Venus is present in the fifth house of the same horoscope in the sign of Pisces, the native may get married to someone well established and well recognized due to which he may witness a rise in his financial as well as social status after his marriage. If benefic Moon is also placed in the fifth house of the same horoscope in the sign of Pisces along with benefic Venus, the native under the combined effect of these benefic influences may get married to a person hailing from a very rich and established family and such native may also get great professional support through his wife and her family.

It means that such native may get married to someone from a rich and established business family and he may get a position of authority in such business of the family of his in-laws, by virtue of his marriage. If benefic Rahu is placed in the eighth house of the same horoscope in the sign of Gemini, the native under the combined effect of benefic retrograde Jupiter in fourth house, benefic Venus and benefic Moon in fifth house and benefic Rahu in eighth house can achieve very good status and a direct share in the family business of such life partner. The combined effect of these benefic influences may either bless the native with a good share of profit in the family business of the life partner or such native may get elevated to a position of power and authority in a political party or even in some state government, on the basis of his marriage to a person belonging to a well established political family.

Benefic retrograde Jupiter in the fourth house of a horoscope can also bless the native in the field of his profession and accordingly some natives under this benefic influence may achieve success through different professional fields and on different levels, depending on the type and strength of this influence as well as depending on the overall tone of their horoscopes. For example, the presence of benefic retrograde Jupiter in the fourth house of a horoscope in the sign of Scorpio can motivate the native to pursue a profession related to some type of defense or security services and accordingly the native may have strong tendencies to follow one such profession. If there are other influences supporting such profession, the native may actively engage in one such profession and he may achieve success through such profession.

For instance, the presence of benefic Mars, benefic Mercury, benefic Sun or benefic Rahu in the sixth house of the same horoscope in the sign of Capricorn can convert such interest of the native into actual practice and accordingly, the native under the combined effect of these benefic planets may engage in a profession related to security or defense. If the overall horoscope of the native is weak and not supportive, the native may become a security guard with some private company or he may also get selected in police or army, on one of the lowest possible direct ranks. However, if there are other good influences in the horoscope of such native, the native may witness much better results related to his profession.

Taking a look at one such combination, the presence of benefic Sun in the first house of a horoscope in the sign of Leo when benefic retrograde Jupiter is placed in fourth house of this horoscope in the sign of Scorpio and benefic Mars or benefic Rahu is placed in the sixth house of this horoscope in the sign of Capricorn can bless the native with success on a much bigger level. Such native may either get selected at a high rank in some department of government that deals with security or defense like police force or army, or such native may run his own security company which provides security guards or other types of security services as well as security equipments.

If benefic Mercury is also placed in the first house of the same horoscope in the sign of Leo, the native under the combined effect of all these benefic planets may get selected in police, army or in some type of administrative service, directly at a very high or even at the highest possible direct rank. As more and more positive influences keep adding to this equation, the professional results achieved by this native may become better and better, like the presence of benefic Rahu in the fourth house of the same horoscope along with benefic retrograde Jupiter can further enhance the professional success achieved by this native. Such native may have a very good career record and he may get many promotions, recognitions and even some formal awards for his extraordinary service to his department.

The presence of benefic retrograde Jupiter in the fourth house of a horoscope can also bless the native with good results in the field of spiritualism and accordingly some natives benefitting from this good influence may witness different type and different quantum of results related to this domain, depending on the type and strength of this placement, as well as depending on the overall tone of their horoscopes. For example, the presence of benefic retrograde Jupiter in the fourth house of a horoscope in the sign of Cancer can create spiritual, paranormal or other such tendencies in the native and accordingly the native may become more and more interested in some of these fields. Such placement of benefic retrograde Jupiter may indicate that the native has actively followed one of these lines in his past lives, particularly in his recent past life and he wants to follow it in this life too.

If benefic Moon, benefic Rahu, benefic Mars, benefic Saturn, benefic Sun or benefic Venus is placed in the twelfth house of the same horoscope in the sign of Pisces or if benefic Rahu, benefic Venus or benefic Sun is present in the eighth house of the same horoscope in the sign of Scorpio, the native may actively follow one such line and he may either become a professional with expertise in one of these lines or he may start researching in one such line as well as start teaching in one such line, after some years of research in the line. For example, the presence of benefic Mars or benefic Rahu in the eighth house of a horoscope in the sign of Scorpio when benefic retrograde Jupiter is present in the fourth house of the same horoscope in the sign of Cancer can make the native pursue a profession related to some type of paranormal or spiritual field and accordingly such native may become a professional astrologer, numerologist, psychic or some other professional of this type.

The native under the combined influence of such benefic retrograde Jupiter in the fourth house and benefic Rahu or benefic Mars in the eighth house of his horoscope may achieve good or very good amount of professional success depending on his overall horoscope. For example, the presence of benefic Sun and benefic Mercury in the tenth house of the same horoscope in the sign of Capricorn can enhance the professional success achieved by such native many times. Accordingly, the native under the combined effect of these benefic influences in various houses of his horoscope may become a successful and famous astrologer, numerologist, vastu expert, psychic or some other professional dealing in some other similar field of profession.

However, the presence of benefic Moon in the twelfth house of a horoscope in the sign of Pisces when benefic retrograde Jupiter is present in the fourth house of the same horoscope in the sign of Cancer can change the entire equation and the native under the combined effect of these two benefic influences may become more interested in the field of spiritualism. Such native may practice and research in some field related to spiritualism and if the overall horoscope allows, he may gain a position of authority in some spiritual organization. For instance, the presence of benefic Sun in the tenth house of the same horoscope can bless the native with a post of high authority and recognition in some spiritual organization which operates on national or on international level.

However, the presence of benefic Sun in the ninth house of a horoscope in sign of Sagittarius when benefic retrograde

Jupiter is placed in fourth house and benefic Moon is placed in the twelfth house of the same horoscope can bless the native either with a post of very high or the highest authority in a big spiritual organization or such native may start his own spiritual organization and he may achieve good amount of success and fame through it. If benefic Rahu or benefic Venus is placed in the tenth house of this horoscope, the native under the combined effect of benefic retrograde Jupiter and other benefic planets which have been already mentioned, may start a new spiritual faith or organization which may gain popularity not on the national level, but on international level also.

On the other hand, malefic retrograde Jupiter in the fourth house of a horoscope can cause problems related to marriage, profession, overall health and many other spheres of a native's life and accordingly some natives suffering from such malefic influence may have to face problems in some spheres of their lives. Such problems may be of different type and different quantum, depending on the type and strength of this malefic placement, as well as depending on the overall tone of the horoscopes of different natives under such malefic influence.

Marriage is one sphere which can be affected seriously if retrograde Jupiter placed in fourth house of a horoscope turns negative and accordingly, some natives under this malefic influence may feel the heat of this bad influence in their marriages. Some natives under such malefic influence may have to wait till late or very late in their lives, in order to get married whereas some other such natives may have to face problems and disturbances in their marriages. For example, the presence of malefic retrograde Jupiter in the fourth house of a horoscope in the sign of Capricorn can cause delay as well as disturbance in the marriage of the native under its influence and accordingly such native may face problems in getting married.

It should be noted that since Jupiter is debilitated in the sign of Capricorn, though such placement of malefic retrograde Jupiter in the fourth house of a horoscope in the sign of Capricorn may cause delay and problems in the marriage of the native under its influence, this malefic influence on its own is not capable of causing long delays or denial of marriage. Such malefic influence is also not capable of causing great disturbances or divorce after the marriage of the native on its own, since such malefic retrograde Jupiter doesn't possess much strength due to debilitation. However, if there are some other malefic influences present in the same horoscope, the effects of such malefic retrograde Jupiter can multiply and accordingly it may cause damage on a much bigger level.

For instance, the presence of malefic Mars in the fourth house of the same horoscope in the sign of Capricorn along with malefic retrograde Jupiter can increase the intensity of the problems many times and accordingly the native under the combined influence of such malefic planets may have to face problems of much higher intensity. This is due to the fact that the presence of malefic but exalted Mars in the fourth house of this horoscope will provide extra strength to the malefic but weak retrograde Jupiter and accordingly, the combined effect of these two malefic planets can cause serious problems in the marriage of the native.

This is a perfect case for study and research for the people interested in astrology as well as for astrologers practicing in it, as this is a case of NeechBhanga Yoga with the opposite effect. It means that though the Neecha status of retrograde Jupiter which is the debilitation status of retrograde Jupiter, is cancelled by virtue of the conjunction of exalted Mars with it, in a Kendra house of this horoscope, the cancellation of such debilitation status doesn't result in a Raj Yoga and instead it results in problems of very high quantum. This is due to the fact that both Mars and retrograde Jupiter involved in this combination are working negatively in this horoscope and the combination of two malefic planets can never give birth to a Raj Yoga. Hence malefic Jupiter gains strength through the company of such malefic exalted Mars and the combined effect of these malefic influences may cause havoc in the marriage and married life of the native, if there are no marriage saving combinations in the horoscope of such native.

Such problems may not only include delay in the marriage of such native, but they may also include serious disturbances in the married life of the native. Accordingly, the native under the combined effect of malefic retrograde Jupiter and malefic Mars in the fourth house of his horoscope in the sign of Capricorn may have to witness one or more than one broken or deeply troubled marriages. The situation can become even worse if a combination of Venus and malefic Saturn, malefic Rahu or malefic Ketu is present in the sixth house of the same horoscope in the sign of Pisces. The native under the combined effect of these malefic influences may have to witness more than one broken marriage after facing great disturbances and troubles in such marriages.

Retrograde Jupiter in 5th House

The placement of retrograde Jupiter in fifth house of a horoscope whether such Jupiter is benefic or malefic, carries great importance for the native as retrograde Jupiter placed in fifth house of a horoscope can not only bless the native with a wide variety of good things in many spheres of his life if such Jupiter is working positively, but it can also trouble the native on almost every front of his life if such Jupiter goes malefic in the fifth house of a horoscope. When working positively in a horoscope, retrograde Jupiter placed in fifth house of a horoscope can render good results to the native related to the spheres of education, marriage, children, profession, finances, health, longevity, wisdom, spiritual growth and many other spheres of his life. Accordingly many natives benefitting from this positive influence may experience good results in many spheres of their lives depending on the type and strength of this placement as well as depending on the overall tone of the horoscopes of these natives.

Such benefic influence in the fifth house of a horoscope can bless the native with very good education and accordingly some natives may witness good or very good results related to the field of their education, right from their early childhood till their higher education. Such benefic influence can bless the native with good memory, good or very good level of intelligence and a good sense of understanding different situations and topics due to which the natives under such benefic influence may perform very well at their studies by virtue of these abilities, compared to other students in the same classes or courses. For example, the presence of benefic retrograde Jupiter in the fifth house of a horoscope in the sign of Gemini can bless the native with very good performance at studies and accordingly such native may achieve very good grades during most of his study period.

If benefic Venus, benefic Mars, benefic Sun, benefic Mercury or benefic Rahu is also placed in the fifth house of the same horoscope in the sign of Gemini, the native under the combined effect of these two benefic planets may perform even better at his studies and he may also receive very good level of higher education on academic level. Such native may pursue his higher education on some topic till the level of Master's degree or even more and he may also get very good results in such education. If benefic retrograde Jupiter is present in the fifth house of a horoscope in the sign of Gemini along with benefic Mercury, and benefic Venus or benefic Rahu is placed in the fourth house of the same horoscope in the sign of Taurus, the native under the combined effect of such benefic influences may achieve a degree of specialization in some specific professional sphere like a degree of mass communication, journalism, business administration, engineering of some type or some other professional degree relevant to the overall theme of his horoscope.

However, if benefic Venus or Rahu is present in the ninth house of the same horoscope in the sign of Libra, the native under the combined effect of such positive influence may go to the highest level of academic studies in some particular field and he may achieve a degree of doctorate on some subject or some other degree parallel to the degree of doctorate. It means that such native may obtain a degree of the highest possible order in some subject of general education or in some subject of specific application. Such native may not only achieve such degree of the highest order in some field, but he may also achieve very good amount of professional success by virtue of such highest class education.

Speaking about profession, benefic retrograde Jupiter placed in the fifth house of a horoscope can bless the native with professional success related to various professional fields and accordingly different natives under this benefic influence may witness success in different professions depending on the type and strength of this placement, as well as depending on their overall horoscopes. For example, the presence of benefic retrograde Jupiter in the fifth house of a horoscope in the sign of Scorpio can motivate the native to pursue higher studies related to the field of medicals and accordingly the native may take much interest in such field, though this placement alone may not be sufficient when it comes to make the native a professional doctor.

Continuing with this benefic placement, if benefic Sun, benefic Mars or benefic Venus is placed in the sixth house of the same horoscope in the sign of Sagittarius when benefic retrograde Jupiter is placed in the fifth house of this horoscope, the native under the combined effect of these benefic influences may obtain a degree of high level in medical field and he may start practicing as a professional doctor. Such native may specialize in some specific field of medical depending on the overall tone of his horoscope and he may also achieve good, very good or great amount of professional success, depending on his overall horoscope. For example, the presence of benefic Sun or benefic Mars in the sixth house of the same horoscope in the sign of Sagittarius can make the native become a specialist surgeon or consultant physician whereas the presence of benefic Rahu in the sixth house of the same horoscope in the sign of Sagittarius can make the native become a specialist neurologist, cardiologist, physiotherapist or psychologist.

The placement of benefic retrograde Jupiter in fifth house of a horoscope in the sign of Pisces can bless the native with certain special abilities related to the fields of spiritualism, paranormal and other such fields, apart from blessing the native with good amount of formal education. Accordingly some natives blessed by this benefic influence may specialize in one of these fields and they may start practicing as professionals in such fields. If benefic Rahu or benefic Venus is placed in the first house of this horoscope in the sign of Scorpio, the native under the combined effect of these benefic planets may become a successful astrologer or he may start providing spiritual guidance to the people in need of it, after gaining good amount of knowledge and experience in the subject.

If benefic Saturn is placed in the eighth house of the same horoscope when benefic retrograde Jupiter is placed in the fifth house and benefic Rahu or benefic Venus is present in the first house of the horoscope, the native under the combined effect of these benefic influences may witness very god amount of professional success as an astrologer or he may start his own organization which teaches people the way of meditation and healing techniques which can be mastered through mediation. Such native may specialize in some specific techniques of meditation or yoga and he may achieve good amount of success and recognition by teaching these techniques to many people, as a good number of people suffering from various physical as well as mental problems may see improvements after trying such techniques. If benefic Moon or benefic Sun is present in ninth house of the same horoscope in the sign of Cancer, the amount of success and recognition obtained by this native may increase further.

Taking a look at another combination in the same case, if benefic retrograde Jupiter is present in the fifth house of a horoscope in the sign of Pisces and benefic Moon is present in the twelfth house of the same horoscope in the sign of Libra, the native under the combined effect of these benefic influences may become more interested in direct spiritual studies and practices, instead of being interested in other faiths like astrology or other such healing techniques. Such native may conduct studies and researches on various spiritual techniques and faiths, and he may start teaching them independently or through some organization of the same kind, after reaching a good level of spiritual progress.

If benefic Venus is present in the ninth house of the same horoscope in the sing of Cancer, the results and progress achieved by the native under the combined influence of such benefic planets may see very good rise and accordingly the native may witness more success in this sphere. Such native may get a post of authority in some spiritual organization and he may also be given the charge of a complete branch of a spiritual organization with the passage of time, under the influence of such benefic retrograde Jupiter and other benefic planets mentioned in this example. Moving ahead, if benefic Rahu or benefic Sun is placed in the tenth house of the same horoscope in the sign of Leo, the native under the combined effect of such benefic influences may become the head of the complete state body of a big spiritual organization or he may start his own spiritual faith or organization which may achieve very good amount of success, with the passage of time.

Benefic retrograde Jupiter in the fifth house of a horoscope can also bless the native with good results related to the children aspect and accordingly some natives under the benefic influence of this placement may witness different type of good things related to their children, depending on the type and strength of this placement as well as depending on the overall tone of the horoscopes of these natives. It should be noted that though some astrologers believe that the placement of Jupiter in fifth house of a horoscope is not a good placement for this planet as it can cause problems related to the children aspect of the native and it can even deprive the native of any children, but such beliefs are just misconceptions and nothing more than that.

It is believed by these astrologers that Jupiter placed in fifth house of a horoscope can cause the effect of 'Karako Bhavo Nashto' which means that if the significator of any house of a horoscope is placed in that house itself, it can destroy the results related to that house. As Jupiter is the significator of the fifth house according to Vedic astrology, it is believed by these astrologers that the presence of Jupiter in fifth house of a horoscope can delay the child birth or it can deny children to such native. However, this is just a misconception and nothing else as such effects can only be caused by Jupiter placed in the fifth house of a horoscope, when such Jupiter is working negatively in the horoscope whereas the presence of benefic Jupiter in the fifth house of a horoscope can bless the native with some of the best possible children, among many other good things.

For example, the presence of benefic retrograde Jupiter in the fifth house of a horoscope in the sign of Cancer can bless the native with beautiful, healthy and intelligent children and accordingly, the natives under the good influence of this placement are likely to be blessed by such children, provided their overall horoscopes allow it. The presence of such benefic retrograde Jupiter in the fifth house of a horoscope in the sign of Cancer is especially very good for the female natives when it comes to conceiving and delivering children. Accordingly the female natives benefitting from this positive influence are likely to have solid reproductive organs as well as good reproductive systems and by virtue of these things, they are able to conceive and deliver children without any major issues. If benefic Moon is also placed in the fifth house of the same horoscope of a female native in the sign of Cancer, such female native may give birth to children with special abilities like creative abilities, and her children may earn good amount of success and fame through such abilities.

On the other hand, the presence of retrograde Jupiter in the fifth house of a horoscope can cause serious problems for the native under its influence if such Jupiter turns negative in a horoscope. Accordingly the natives suffering from such malefic influence may face problems and disturbances in many spheres of their lives depending on the type and strength of such malefic placement, as well as depending on their overall horoscopes. Some natives under the malefic effect of this bad influence may face difficulty and delay in child birth and they may have to wait till long or very long period of time in order to have their first child, whereas some other natives under this malefic influence may give birth to children who are physically or mentally not up to the normal standard and they may also have some physical or mental disabilities in some extreme cases of this malefic influence.

Such malefic retrograde Jupiter in fifth house may especially be very bad when it happens to be in the horoscope of a female and accordingly some female natives under such malefic influence may have to face different types of problems related to child birth, depending on the type and strength of such malefic influence and depending on the overall tone of their horoscope. For example, the presence of malefic retrograde Jupiter in the fifth house of the horoscope of a female in the sign of Scorpio can trouble her a lot when it comes to conceive and deliver children. Such female native may suffer from some defect related to one of her reproductive organs like uterus or ovaries, or the working of such organs may not be normal due to which she may have difficulties in conceiving. Such female native may have to face delay in conceiving her first child and she may also have to go through medical treatment in order to conceive a child.

If malefic Rahu, malefic Ketu or malefic Saturn is also placed in fifth house of the same horoscope along with malefic retrograde Jupiter in the sign of Scorpio, the female native under the combined effect of these malefic planets may have to face problems of higher intensity. Such female native may have to face abortion of one or more than one of her child and in some extreme cases, she may have to face medical complications or even a possible threat to her life by virtue of an abortion causing poisoning effect in her body. The combined effect of such malefic influences may also delay the child birth till a very long age and in some extreme cases, when there are no child promoting factors, such female native may have to remain childless throughout her life.

For example, the combination of malefic retrograde Jupiter and malefic Rahu or Ketu in the fifth house of the horoscope of a female native in the sign of Scorpio can cause abortions and medical complications whereas the presence of a combination of malefic retrograde Jupiter and malefic Saturn in the fifth house of the same horoscope can cause very long delay in childbirth and such combination can also deny the possibility of a children forever, if there are no child promoting combinations present in the horoscope of such female native. For instance, the presence of benefic Moon and benefic Venus in the first house of the same horoscope in this sign of Cancer can still bless this female native with one or even more than one child after some delay and some medical treatment, despite the presence of such malefic combination in the fifth house of her horoscope.

Malefic retrograde Jupiter in fifth house can also cause problems related to the professional sphere of the native and accordingly some natives under such bad influence may have to face negative results related to their professional spheres where the type and intensity of these negative results may vary from native to native, depending on the type and strength of this placement, as well as depending on the overall tone of the horoscope of the native in question. Some natives under this malefic influence may not get jobs according to their qualifications and they may have to work for jobs which pay low or much low compared to their qualifications whereas some other natives under this malefic influence may have to remain jobless for periods of some months or even some years, more than once in their lives. In extreme cases, when such malefic retrograde Jupiter in fifth house of a horoscope is strong and the overall horoscope is also negative, the native may not be able to get a stable profession till late in his life or for his entire life and he may have to live on support of his relatives and friends.

Retrograde Jupiter in 6th House

When benefic in nature, retrograde Jupiter placed in sixth house of a horoscope can bless the native with professional success, good health, long life, education, wisdom and many other good things where the type and quantum of good results experienced by different natives under this influence may be different depending on the type and strength of this placement as well as depending on the overall tone of the horoscopes of these natives. Benefic retrograde Jupiter in sixth house can render success to the native under its influence through a variety of professions and accordingly some natives under this benefic influence may achieve success through different professional spheres. For example, the presence of benefic retrograde Jupiter in the sixth house of a horoscope in the sign of Libra can motivate the native to pursue his higher studies in law and accordingly such native may be interested in becoming a professional lawyer though this placement on its own may not be sufficient to make the native a professional lawyer.

If benefic Mars, benefic Mercury, benefic Saturn or benefic Rahu is also placed in the sixth house of the same horoscope in the sign of Libra, the native under the combined effect of these benefic influences may pursue his higher studies in law and he may start practicing as a professional lawyer. The type of practice this native engages in as well as the amount of success achieved by him depends on the overall tone of his horoscope as well as on the planet or planets which are present with retrograde Jupiter, in the sixth house of his horoscope in the sign of Libra. For example, if Mars is present in the sixth house of this horoscope in the sign of Libra, the native under the combined effect of these two benefic planets may practice as a criminal lawyer and he is likely to achieve an average level of success if there are no other benefic influences in the horoscope of the native.

However, if instead of benefic Mars, benefic Mercury is placed in the sixth house of this horoscope in the sign of Libra, the combined effect of such benefic retrograde Jupiter and benefic Mercury in the sixth house of this horoscope in the sign of Libra can bless the native with good amount of success and such native may either become a well recognized lawyer of a city court or he may practice in some higher court of law like a court dealing with the affairs of an entire state. If benefic Saturn also joins this combination of benefic retrograde Jupiter and benefic Mercury in the sixth house of the same horoscope in the sign of Libra, the amount of success achieved by native may increase many times. Accordingly the native under the combined effect of these benefic influences may practice in some higher court of law and he may earn very good amount of money as well as recognition through his practice of law.

If benefic Venus or benefic Rahu is also present in the sixth house of the same horoscope along with benefic retrograde Jupiter, Mercury and Saturn in the sign of Libra, the native under the combined effect of these benefic influences may achieve phenomenal success as a lawyer. Such native may practice in a high or in the highest court of law of his country and he may earn very good amount of money and fame through such practice. The presence of benefic Rahu in the sixth house of this horoscope along with the other three benefic planets can make the native famous on national level and he may charge very high fee for appearing in court, on behalf of his clients. In other words, the native may become a lawyer of the richest and the most powerful people of his country.

On the other hand, the presence of benefic Venus in the sixth house of this horoscope along with benefic retrograde Jupiter, Mercury and Saturn in the sign of Libra can not only bless the native with great amount of success through this profession, but such benefic combination of these four planets can also bless the native with the post of a judge in some higher court of law. Such native is likely to practice as a lawyer for some years and then he may get elevated as a judge in some higher court of law, provided there are no opposing combinations in his horoscope. If benefic Moon or benefic Rahu is placed in the tenth house of the same horoscope in the sign of Aquarius, the combined effect of these five planets can bless the native either with the post of chief justice of a state court, or it can bless him with the post of a judge in the highest court of law of his country.

Benefic retrograde Jupiter in sixth house of a horoscope can also bless the native with success through politics and accordingly some natives benefitting from this placement may witness success through politics. The amount of success achieved by different natives under this benefic influence as well as the time taken by them to achieve this success may vary from native to native depending on the type and strength of this benefic placement, as well as depending on the overall tone of the horoscopes of these natives. For example, the presence of benefic retrograde Jupiter in the sixth house of a horoscope in the sign of Leo can make the native interested in politics and accordingly the native may plan for a career in politics, though such placement alone may not be sufficient on its own to produce significant results related to this field.

However, if benefic Sun is also present in the sixth house of the same horoscope, the combined effect of such benefic retrograde Jupiter and benefic Sun in the sixth house of this horoscope in the sign of Leo can make the native become an active politician. The native under the combined effect of these two benefic planets may achieve good amount of success through politics, like he may become a well recognized politician of his city, provided his overall horoscope allows it. The presence of benefic Mercury in the sixth house of the same horoscope can further enhance the results and accordingly the native under the combined effect of these three benefic planets may achieve even more success through politics.

Such native may not only become a successful politician on a city level, but he may also become a leader on the state level and he may achieve good amount of success also, as a state leader. The combined effect of such benefic retrograde Jupiter, benefic Sun and benefic Mercury in the sixth house of this horoscope in the sign of Leo can also bless the native with an election ticket from a well established political party, where such ticket may belong to an election on state level which is the state assembly. However, the combined influence of such benefic planets alone may not be sufficient when it comes to win such election and represent an area of a state in the assembly of that state, and the native may need more benefic influences in his horoscope to achieve this goal.

Talking about these influences, the presence of benefic Moon, benefic Mars, benefic Venus or benefic Rahu in the fourth house of this horoscope in the sign of Gemini can bless the native with win in one or more than one such election. Accordingly, the native under the combined effect of benefic retrograde Jupiter, Sun and Mercury in the sixth house of his horoscope and one of the above mentioned benefic planets say Rahu in the fourth house of his horoscope may win such elections more than once. Such native may not only become a member of legislative assembly of a state more than once, but the combined effect of these benefic influences can also bless him with a ministry in the state government. If benefic

Moon or benefic Mars is present in the tenth house of the same horoscope in the sign of Sagittarius, the combined effect of all these planets in various houses of the horoscope can bless this native with important ministries in a state government more than once in his life. As more and more variables keep adding to the equation, such native may achieve more or less amount of success in his political career.

On the other hand, retrograde Jupiter can prove to be one of the worst placements of this planet in a horoscope, if it turns negative when placed in sixth house of a horoscope. Accordingly many natives under the bad influence of such malefic retrograde Jupiter in the sixth house of their horoscopes may suffer on different fronts of their lives where the problems faced by such natives and the intensity of these problems depend on the type and strength of this malefic influence as well as on the overall tone of the horoscopes of these natives.

Malefic retrograde Jupiter in sixth house of a horoscope can cause problems related to professional and financial sphere of the native under its influence and accordingly some natives suffering from this bad influence may have to face many problems related to their profession and overall financial situation. For example, the presence of malefic retrograde Jupiter in the sixth house of a horoscope in the sing of Leo can make the native struggle a lot on his professional front and accordingly the native under this malefic influence may have to put in much effort and he may also have to wait till late or very late in his life in order to witness even reasonably good professional results. This is the beauty of astrology how the same retrograde Jupiter placed in sixth house of a horoscope in the sign of Leo can bless the native with top class success in profession when it is working positively in the horoscope whereas the same placement of retrograde Jupiter in the same house and same sign can cause many problems for the native, related to his professional sphere, when it is working negatively in the horoscope.

The presence of malefic Rahu, malefic Ketu or malefic Saturn in the sixth house of the same horoscope in the sign of Leo can further deteriorate this equation and accordingly the native suffering from such malefic combination of malefic retrograde Jupiter and one more malefic planet say Ketu in the sixth house of his horoscope may have to suffer a lot, in relation to his professional sphere. The native under the combined influence of these two malefic planets may have to keep struggling for professional success, till late in his life or he may not be able to establish himself professionally, throughout his life if there are some other malefic influences present in his horoscope, which impact his profession in a negative way. For instance, if malefic Saturn is placed in the tenth house of the same horoscope in the sign of Sagittarius, the native under the combined effect of these malefic planets in sixth and tenth house of his horoscope may have to work for low or very low paying jobs and he may not even be able to earn enough to live a decent life.

The combined effect of such malefic influences can also cause serious problems related to the financial aspect of the native and the native may have to face serious financial problems many times in his life or throughout his life if there are no other good combinations in his horoscope which promote financial growth. It should be noted that professional aspect and overall financial aspect of a native are two different things and they should not be understood as one. The professional aspect of a native relates to the level of success as well as money earned through his profession whereas the overall financial aspect includes his overall finances which include his professional income, gifts, lotteries, financial support from relatives and friends, and some other types of financial incomes. Hence a native may not earn much from his profession but he may still have a very good financial equation by virtue of belonging to a rich family, by virtue of support from his relatives or friends, or by virtue of some other means which can keep providing him with money from time to time.

Coming back to the point, the combined effect of such malefic retrograde Jupiter and malefic Ketu in the sixth house of a horoscope in the sign of Leo and malefic Saturn in the tenth house of the same horoscope in the sign of Sagittarius can trouble the native on the front of overall financial equation also. Such native may have to face financial crisis and he may have to avail financial loans many times in his life due to the combined effect of these malefic planets. If there are some other malefic influences in the horoscope of the native, he may have to face legal actions also, due to non-payment of one or more than one such financial loan.

For example, the presence of malefic Sun in the second house of the same horoscope in the sign of Aries can intensify the problems faced by this native. Accordingly, the native under the combined effect of these malefic influences may not be able to pay his financial debts and he may have to face court cases due to this reason. If there are no other grace saving combinations in his horoscope, the native under the effect of such malefic influences may have to spend some time in prison, by virtue of a court decision going against him.

Malefic retrograde Jupiter in the sixth house of a horoscope can also trouble the native on account of health related issues and accordingly some natives under this malefic influence may have to suffer on account of various health related problems as well as diseases from time to time. Such diseases and their intensity may differ from native to native depending on the type and strength of this malefic influence as well as depending on the overall horoscope of the native in question.

For example, the presence of malefic retrograde Jupiter in the sixth house of a horoscope in the sign of Aries can trouble the native with many health related issues from time to time and if there are some other malefic influences in his horoscope, he may get afflicted with some permanent disease.

For instance, the presence of malefic Venus or Rahu in the sixth house of the same horoscope in the sign of Aries can trouble the native with a permanent disease like diabetes which may only be treated and which may not be cured throughout his life. Hence the native having such malefic combination of retrograde Jupiter and malefic Rahu in the sixth house of his horoscope in the sign of Aries may have to suffer a lot from time to time, by virtue of such disease. If malefic Mars or malefic Mercury is also placed in the sixth house of the same horoscope, the native under the combined effect of these malefic influences may get afflicted with an even more serious disease and accordingly, he may have to suffer much more by virtue of such disease.

Exploring more options, the presence of malefic Sun in the eighth house of the same horoscope in the sign of Gemini can further intensify the problems of this native and the native under the combined effect of all these malefic planets may get afflicted by some life threatening disease which may claim his life at a relatively young age, after troubling him a lot for many years. Apart from this, malefic retrograde Jupiter in sixth house of a horoscope can also trouble the native on account of problems related to children, marriage and many other spheres of his life.

Retrograde Jupiter in 7th House

Retrograde Jupiter placed in the seventh house of a horoscope can render good results related to many spheres of native's life under its influence, if such retrograde Jupiter is benefic in nature. Accordingly different natives benefitting from this positive placement may experience its good results in different spheres of their lives as well as with different quantum depending on the type and strength of this placement as well as depending on the overall tone of their horoscopes. The natives under this benefic influence may see good results in the field of their profession, marriage, status, overall reputation, fame and many other spheres of their lives.

As seventh house of a horoscope directly represents the affairs related to marriage and married life, the presence of benefic retrograde Jupiter in the seventh house of a horoscope can give good, very good or great results related to the marriage of the native, depending on his overall horoscope. Some natives under this benefic influence may get very devoted and dedicated type of life partners who may add much value to their marriages as well as to their lives whereas some other natives having this positive influence may be blessed with wise, well established, foreign settled or some other type of life partners with some other type of good qualities. For example, the presence of benefic retrograde Jupiter in the seventh house of a horoscope in the sign of Pisces can bless the native with a beautiful, caring and devoted life partner and accordingly such native may get married to one such person.

The presence of such benefic retrograde Jupiter in the seventh house of a horoscope of a male can bless him with a wife who is beautiful, caring and devoted, not only to the native and to the marriage, but also to the whole concept of family. It means that such wife may not only take good care of the native and his needs but she may also take good care of his close relatives, friends and other such people due to which, the social status as well as social reputation of the native may rise after marriage, as more and more of his relatives and friends start giving him more value by virtue of the good deeds done by his wife. If benefic Moon is also present in the seventh house of the same horoscope in the sign of Pisces, the native under the combined effect of these benefic planets may get even more benefits through his marriage.

In this case, the native may not only get married to a beautiful and devoted female who adds social and personal value to his life, but such wife may also be financially well established or she may belong to a rich family or she may otherwise bring good luck to the native. Accordingly, the financial status of the native may go higher or much higher after his marriage due to one or the other reasons mentioned in this example. If benefic Rahu, benefic Venus or benefic Mercury is placed in the eighth house of the same horoscope in the sign of Aries, the native under the combined effect of such benefic planets may get married to a female belonging to a rich and established family and he may get good amount of financial as well as professional support from his in-laws. Accordingly such native may witness a rise in his professional as well as in his overall financial equation after marriage.

The presence of such benefic retrograde Jupiter in the seventh house of the horoscope of a female in the sign of Pisces can bless her with a wise, educated and well behaved husband who may not only take good care of her needs but who may also be capable of guiding and helping her on every important front of her life. Such husband serves more like a father figure for this female native as he influences all important decisions of her life in a positive way and he supports her with all his heart and efforts as and when she needs such support. If benefic Moon is also placed in the seventh house of the same horoscope in the sign of Pisces or if benefic Venus is placed in the fifth house of the same horoscope in the sign of Capricorn, such female native under the combined effect of these benefic influences may also get very good benefits related to children, through this marriage. It means that she may be blessed with beautiful and healthy children who may not only possess good amount of courage and confidence, but who may also be blessed with good amount of intelligence and with some creative abilities.

Considering another possibility, the presence of benefic retrograde Jupiter in the seventh house of a horoscope in the sign of Taurus can get the native married to someone belonging to a foreign culture or someone belonging to a foreign country, which means that the life partner of such native may either hail from a foreign country or such life partner may belong to the same background as that of the native but he or she may be settled in a foreign country. Hence the native may himself go to a foreign country and settle their after his marriage and by virtue of his marriage. If benefic Venus is present in the ninth house of the same horoscope in the sign of Cancer or if benefic Rahu is placed in the twelfth house of the same horoscope in the sign of Libra, the native under the combined effect of these benefic planets may not only get married and settled in a foreign country, but he may also witness good amount of professional success, much improved financial equation and rise in overall standard of living, by virtue of such marriage and such settlement in some foreign country.

The presence of benefic retrograde Jupiter in the seventh house of a horoscope in the sign of Leo can bless the native with a life partner who is well established and who may also belong to a rich or well established family. Such benefic influence in the horoscope of a female native may bless her with a husband who may either have a well established profession or who may belong to a well established family which supports him. If benefic Sun is also present in the seventh house of the same horoscope of a female in the sign of Leo, such female native may get married to someone who holds a post of power and authority in some government or in some private organization. If the overall horoscope of such female is supportive, she may enjoy a good part of such power and authority by virtue of her marriage, like the presence of benefic Rahu, benefic Venus, benefic Mars or benefic Saturn in the tenth house of the same horoscope in the sign of Scorpio can bless her with a good part of such power and authority through such marriage.

Benefic retrograde Jupiter in seventh house of a horoscope can also bless the native with professional success and accordingly many natives blessed by this influence may achieve success in different professions and the level of such success may also be different in case of these different natives, depending on the type and strength of this placement as well as depending on the overall tone of the horoscopes of these natives. Some natives under this benefic influence may start their own businesses or practices of some type and they may achieve good or very good amount of success through such businesses or practices, provided their overall horoscopes allow it. For example, the presence of benefic retrograde Jupiter in the seventh house of a horoscope in the sign of Sagittarius can motivate the native to start his own business or some type of practice, though this placement may not be sufficient on its own to materialize this plan.

If benefic Sun is also present in the seventh house of the same horoscope in the sign of Sagittarius, the native under the combined effect of these benefic planets may start some business of his own or he may become a lawyer, a coach, a trainer, a teacher or an instructor of some type depending on the overall tone of his horoscope. If benefic Mercury or benefic Moon is also present in the seventh house of the same horoscope, the amount of success achieved by this native may further increase and he may witness very good amount of financial incomes as well as recognition through some business of his own or through some type of independent practice like the ones already mentioned.

The addition of more positive planets in this equation can bless the native with even more success and profits through his profession whereas the addition of more negative planets in this equation can spoil the good results given by the already mentioned benefic planets. For example, the presence of benefic Rahu or benefic Saturn in the tenth house of the same horoscope in the sign of Pisces can further enhance the good results and accordingly the native may earn even more profits and fame through one of the already mentioned professional spheres. On the other hand, the presence of a combination of malefic Saturn and Malefic Rahu or the presence of a combination of malefic Saturn and Malefic Ketu in the eleventh house of the same horoscope can reduce the professional success achieved by this native considerably. Accordingly this native may not be able to earn much through his profession, despite being blessed by the presence of a very good planetary combination in the seventh house of his horoscope.

All is not well with this placement of retrograde Jupiter in the seventh house of a horoscope and it can cause many problems for the native under its influence if it turns negative in a horoscope, when placed in the seventh house. Accordingly the natives under its malefic influences may have to feel the heat of this bad influence in many spheres of their lives including marriage, profession and overall lifespan. The type of bad results faced by different natives suffering from this malefic influence as well as the intensity of those bad results varies from native to native depending on the type and strength of this placement, as well as depending on the overall tone of the horoscopes of different natives.

Malefic retrograde Jupiter in seventh house is a bad placement for the marriage aspect of the native under its influence and accordingly some natives suffering from this bad influence may witness bad results related to their marriages. Some of these natives may not be able to get married till late or very late in their lives, some of these natives may have to face disturbed marriages or even divorces and some of these natives may have to witness the death of their life partner, depending on the important factors in their horoscopes. For example, the presence of malefic retrograde Jupiter in the seventh house of a horoscope in the sign of Aquarius can delay the marriage of the native and accordingly the native under such malefic influence may have to wait till late in his life, in order to get married.

If malefic Venus or malefic Saturn is placed in the eighth house of the same horoscope in the sign of Pisces, the marriage of this native may be delayed further and he may have to wait till very late in his life, in order to get married. A combination of malefic retrograde Jupiter in the seventh house of a horoscope in the sign of Aquarius and malefic Saturn in the eighth house of the same horoscope in the sign of Pisces can prove even more difficult in case of female natives and this combination can do much more damage in the horoscope of a female compared to the damage done by this malefic combination in the horoscope of a male native. Accordingly the female native under the malefic influence of this combination may have to wait till 35 years of her age or even more, in order to get married and the quality of her marriage whenever she gets married, may also be far below the average, due to the malefic influence of this combination.

It should be noted that though Jupiter is considered to be a generally benefic planet for everyone and the presence of this planet in the seventh house of a horoscope is said to bless the native with very good results related to his or her marriage including a timely marriage, the placement of negative Jupiter in seventh house of a horoscope can cause much or very much damage to the marriage of the native under its influence. This once again proves that the general nature of every planet among navagraha doesn't matter much when it comes to predict the good or bad results given by such planet to the native under its influence, and the specific working nature of every planet in a horoscope is what matters the most. It means that even the planets generally considered as the most benefic planets can render very bad results to a native when they are working negatively in his horoscope and even the planets generally considered as the most malefic ones can bless the native with very good results in one sphere of his life or the other when they are working positively in his horoscope.

Coming back to the example, if malefic Ketu is present in seventh or eighth house of the same horoscope of a female, when malefic retrograde Jupiter is placed in the seventh house of her horoscope in the sign of Aquarius and malefic Saturn is placed in the eighth house of her horoscope in the sign of Pisces, the results produced by this malefic combination of three malefic planets can be disastrous as far as the marriage aspect of this female native is concerned. Such female native under the combined malefic influence of these malefic planets may not get married at all, throughout her life, if there is no strong marriage promoting combination in her horoscope. Speaking about such benefic combinations, the presence of benefic Rahu and benefic Venus in the first house of the horoscope of this female in the sign of Leo can still get her married after some delay, despite the presence of such malefic marriage denying combinations in her horoscope.

Considering another example, the presence of malefic retrograde Jupiter in the seventh house of a horoscope in the sing of Sagittarius can cause different type of problems related to the marriage of the native. Such negative influence may not cause any delays in the marriage of the native and accordingly the native may get married at a proper age, but such malefic influence can cause many problems in the married life of the native. The native under such malefic influence may not enjoy a happy marriage and in fact he may have to face problems in his marriage, particularly the problems related to physical incompatibility between him and his life partner, let's say his wife. It means that though the native may have a healthy sexual appetite or more than a healthy sexual appetite, his wife may have a below average or much below average type of sexual appetite.

As a result, the couple may start lacking physical compatibility soon after the marriage as the native has strong physical needs whereas his wife doesn't bother much about satisfying those needs as she herself has only a little interest for such physical relations. Hence the tension may start rising between this couple due to both of them having different tastes for physical pleasure and such tension can cause some serious damages if there are some other negative influences present in the horoscope of such native. For example, if malefic Moon or malefic Venus is present in the twelfth house of the same horoscope, the native under the combined effect of such malefic retrograde Jupiter in the seventh house of his horoscope in the sign of Sagittarius and malefic Moon in the twelfth house of his horoscope in the sign of Taurus may get involved in an extramarital love affair.

Such extramarital love affair is primarily initiated by the native as he is physically not satisfied with his with his wife and he finally decides to fulfill his physical appetite through an extramarital affair, after keeping such physical urges under as much control as he can. Hence the combined effect of such malefic influences can add another female to the equation and such extramarital affair of the native may become dangerous for marriage if there are some other negative influences in the horoscope of the native, which indicate a breakup or a divorce in his first marriage.

For instance, the presence of malefic Venus or malefic Rahu in the second house of the same horoscope in the sign of Cancer can cause even more problems and accordingly the native under the combined effect of such malefic retrograde Jupiter, malefic Moon and malefic Venus or Rahu in the already mentioned houses of his horoscope may have to face a broken marriage. The native under the combined effect of these malefic planets may get divorced from his wife after a long history of disturbances, drama, arguments and fights; and the native may then get married to the female, with whom he was involved in an extramarital affair.

However, if there is some marriage saving combination in the horoscope of this native, he may get involved in an extramarital affair which may threaten his marriage for some time, but he may then finally come out of such extramarital affair and continue with the same marriage. For instance, if benefic Moon is placed in seventh house of the same horoscope in the sign of Sagittarius along with malefic retrograde Jupiter, instead of being present in the twelfth house of this horoscope, the native may get involved in an extramarital affair but he may finally be able to come out of it and continue his marriage.

Apart from this, malefic retrograde Jupiter in seventh house of a horoscope can also trouble the native with problems in his profession as well as the problems related to his health. Accordingly some natives under this malefic influence may have to witness various types of health issues and professional problems where the type and intensity of such problems may vary from native to native depending on the type and strength of this malefic influence as well as depending on the overall tone of the horoscopes of different natives. In extreme cases, when such malefic retrograde Jupiter is strong and there are some other malefic influences present in the horoscope of such native, it can cause a serious problems related to the professional sphere of the native or it can afflict the native with some life threatening disease which may claim his life, after torturing him for many years.

Retrograde Jupiter in 8th House

When benefic in nature, retrograde Jupiter placed in eighth house of a horoscope can bless the native with a wide variety of good results related to the spheres of his marriage, profession, overall health, spiritualism and many other spheres of his life. Accordingly many natives benefitting from this positive influence may witness good results which can be of different type and different quantum, depending on the type and strength of this benefic placement as well as depending on the overall tone of the horoscopes of these natives. Benefic retrograde Jupiter in eighth house of a horoscope is a very good placement of this planet when it comes to bless the native with professional success, good or very good amount of money and wealth, good marriage, long age, spiritual progress and many other good things.

Benefic retrograde Jupiter in eighth house of a horoscope can bless the native with good, very good or great amount of money as well as other types of wealth which is not directly earned by the native through his profession and which comes to him through some other means. It means that such money and wealth may be passed on to him by his parents or grandparents by means of inheritance or it may come to the native by virtue of some lottery, jackpot or some other such type of instant phenomenon which is not related to the income through his direct profession but which can still make the native have good, very good or great amount of money in a short or very short period of time.

Some of these natives may also gain good or very good amount of money through gifts and other types of financial help that they may receive through their friends or relatives from time to time whereas some other natives under this benefic influence may receive such money and wealth through their spouses or their families. It means that such natives may get married to rich people or people belonging to a rich family and such family may keep helping these natives with money and other resources from time to time, under various contexts. For example, if benefic retrograde Jupiter is present in the eighth house of a horoscope in the sign of Aries, the native may receive good or very good amount of money and other types of wealth which comes to him as an inheritance from his father.

The native under the benefic effect of such retrograde Jupiter may also receive such money and wealth by virtue of a will executed by someone else in his close family, like the maternal grandparents of the native may leave money and wealth for the native where the quantum of such money and wealth depends on the overall tone of the horoscope of the native. If benefic Mars, benefic Rahu or benefic Venus is placed in the second house of the same horoscope in the sign of Libra, the amount of money and wealth received by such native may increase considerably and accordingly this native under the combined effect of these benefic planets may receive considerable amount of money and wealth left by his father or by some other close family member from his father's side like paternal grandfather or from his mother's side like maternal grandfather.

Let's consider one more possibility in the same case and let's consider that a combination of benefic retrograde Jupiter and benefic Mercury is present in the eighth house of a horoscope in the sign of Aries. Such a benefic combination of these two planets can make the native receive very good amount of money through his father or grandfather and such money may come at a time when it is not expected much and such money can change the financial status of the native to a great extent. If benefic Rahu or benefic Moon is also present in the eighth house of the same horoscope in the sign of Aries, the native under the combined effect of such benefic retrograde Jupiter, benefic Mercury and one more benefic planet say benefic Moon may receive very good or even great amount of money through some type of inheritance which may come as a surprise.

For example, the native under the combined effect of these influences may suddenly receive this news that the government of his state or country had acquired a big piece of land which was owned by his grandfather who died years back, and the government didn't pay the justified price for that piece of land, according to the opinion of his grandfather. Hence his grandfather filed a case in a court of law that he was entitled to much more money than what was paid to him. Such court case keeps going and though the grandfather dies, but the case keeps proceeding. All of a sudden, when the right type of time comes, the native under the benefic effect of such retrograde Jupiter, Mercury and Moon in the eighth house of his horoscope may come to know that they have won the case and a very big amount of money has been awarded to the legal heirs of his grandfather by a court of law, as a settlement for the case filed by his grandfather.

The native may be the only heir to such money which means he may be the only son of the only son of his grandfather or he may have some other heirs in the family who are entitled to an equal share in the money awarded by such court of law. In any case, the native may receive very big amount of money through such court decision and such money may raise the financial status of the native considerably, thereby changing the future course of his life. If benefic Rahu or benefic Venus is placed in the eleventh house of the same horoscope in the sign of Cancer, the native under the combined effect of these four benefic planets may receive very big amount of money, wealth as well as some well established business by means of inheritance, provided his overall horoscope allows all this.

Looking at one more such possibility in the same case, if a combination of benefic retrograde Jupiter, benefic Mercury and benefic Rahu is present in the eighth house of a horoscope in the sign of Aries, the native under the combined effect of these benefic planets may not only receive big amount of money by means of an inheritance left by one of his family members, but he may also receive such money through a will executed by someone who is not related to the native at all. Such native may develop a bond of love with someone rich or very rich and such bond of love may keep getting stronger and stronger with each passing day.

Such rich person may not have any legal heir of his own choice in his direct family and as a result, he may leave a big part of his wealth and property to the native, by means of a will. If there are other benefic influences present in the horoscope of the native in the same case, the native under the combined effect of such benefic retrograde Jupiter and other benefic planets in the eighth house of his horoscope may receive the entire wealth and property of a very rich person through his will, where such wealth may amount to multi-millions or even to billions, depending on the overall horoscope of the native.

Eighth house of a horoscope is generally considered as a very bad or even the worst house of a horoscope by many astrologers and such astrologers believe that the placement of any planet in the eighth house of a horoscope can only result in bad things happening to the native. This is just a misconception and the truth may be quite the opposite to this belief in some cases as eighth house of a horoscope is undoubtedly one of the most resourceful houses of a horoscope and this house has the potential of blessing the native with a number of good things related to many spheres of his life, if the planet or planets placed in this house of the horoscope are benefic and the overall tone of the horoscope of the native under consideration is supportive.

The beauty of the eighth house of a horoscope is that it can render greatest of the results to the native, in the shortest possible time, compared to almost any other house of a horoscope. Hence the planetary influences in this house of the horoscope as well as the overall working of planetary lord of this house and the general significator for this house should be studied carefully before concluding all the malefic results related to the planets placed in this house. The truth may be quite the opposite in some cases and the native may achieve so many good things in his life through the eighth house of his horoscope.

Moving on, benefic retrograde Jupiter in the eighth house of a horoscope can also render good, very good or great amount of professional success to the native under its influence and accordingly different natives under this benefic influence may achieve success through different types of professional spheres depending on the type and strength of the benefic influence as well as depending on the overall tone of their horoscopes. The number of professional spheres through which such benefic retrograde Jupiter can render success to the native is countless as this benefic placement can bless the native with success through a great number of professions. Some natives under such benefic influence may become officers with banks or some other financial institutions and they may earn good amount of money and recognition through their jobs.

For example, the presence of benefic retrograde Jupiter in the eighth house of a horoscope in the sign of Aquarius can bless the native with success through one such field and accordingly the native under the effect of such benefic influence may become an officer with some bank or with some financial institution. If benefic Rahu or benefic Saturn is also placed in the eighth house of the same horoscope in the sign of Aquarius, the combined effect of these benefic planets can increase the amount of success achieved by the native and accordingly the native may get a post of high status and authority in some bank or in some other financial institution. The career graph of such native may show steady growth and he may keep rising higher and higher in his professional sphere, throughout his life, provided his overall horoscope supports all this.

If benefic Venus, benefic Sun, benefic Mars or benefic Moon is placed in the tenth house of the same horoscope in the sign of Aries, the native under the combined effect of all these benefic planets may see even higher level of good results through such profession, where such results may be different in different cases, depending on the planet present in the tenth house of this horoscope as well as depending on the overall tone of his horoscope. For example, if benefic Sun is present in the tenth house of a horoscope in the sign of Aries when a combination of benefic retrograde Jupiter and benefic Saturn or Rahu is placed in the eighth house of the same horoscope in the sign of Aquarius, the native may achieve a post of much higher status and authority, under the combined influence of these benefic planets. Such native may become a high authority in the state unit of a national or even an international bank, at a relatively young age. As more positive variables keep adding to this equation, the good results achieved by this native keep increasing in number as well as in quantum.

Apart from this, benefic retrograde Jupiter in the eighth house of a horoscope can render success through many other professional spheres, to the native under its influence and accordingly some natives under this benefic influence may achieve success through different professional spheres depending on their overall horoscopes. The presence of benefic retrograde Jupiter in the eighth house of a horoscope can also bless the native with good results related to his marriage and accordingly different natives benefitting from this good influence may witness different types of good results through their marriages, depending on their overall horoscopes. Such benefic influence can also render good, very good or great amount of special abilities related to the fields of spiritualism, paranormal and other such spheres, to the native under its impact. Accordingly, some natives under such benefic influence may see progress in these spheres also and some of them may engage in one of these fields on professional basis, if their overall horoscopes allow such practices.

On the other hand, malefic retrograde Jupiter placed in eighth house of a horoscope can cause countless number of problems and troubles to the native under its influence where such troubles can come through the sphere of his marriage, profession, financial status, health, lifespan and many other spheres of his life. Accordingly, some natives suffering from this malefic influence may witness bad results in many spheres of their lives where such results can change in nature and quantum in case of different natives, depending on the type and strength of such malefic retrograde Jupiter, as well as depending on the overall tone of the horoscopes of these natives.

Though malefic retrograde Jupiter in the eighth house of a horoscope can trouble the native in almost any sphere of his life, this placement is especially very bad for the marriage aspect of the native. Accordingly some natives under this malefic influence may witness different types of problems related to their marriages, like some natives under such bad influence may not get married till late or very late in their lives whereas some other natives suffering from such negative retrograde Jupiter may have to face great disturbances and troubles in their marriages. In extreme cases, when such malefic influence is strong and it is supported by some other negative planets in a horoscope, it can either deny the possibility of marriage to a native or it can cause more than one broken marriage.

Looking at some practical examples, the presence of malefic retrograde Jupiter in the eighth house of a horoscope in the sign of Virgo can cause delay in the marriage of the native and accordingly the native under such malefic influence may get married late in his life. Such malefic placement of retrograde Jupiter in eighth house of a horoscope in the sign of Virgo is even worse if it happens to be in the horoscope of a female and accordingly the female native suffering from this malefic influence may have to face even more intense negative results related to her marriage. The female native under this malefic influence may not be able to get married at a proper time and she may have to wait long in order to get married.

If malefic Saturn, malefic Ketu or malefic Mercury is placed in the seventh house of the same horoscope in the sign of Leo, the problems of such female may intensify even more. Accordingly, the female native under the combined effect of such malefic retrograde Jupiter in the eighth house of her horoscope in the sign of Virgo and malefic Saturn, Ketu or Mercury, let's say malefic Saturn in the seventh house of her horoscope may have to wait till 35 years of her life or even longer in order to get married. If malefic Ketu is also present in the eighth house of the same horoscope along with malefic retrograde Jupiter in the sign of Virgo or if a combination of malefic Sun and malefic Mercury is present in the ninth house of the same horoscope in the sign of Libra, the female native under the combined effect of such malefic influences may not get married at all throughout her life despite her best efforts, provided there are no other marriage promoting combinations present in her horoscope.

Speaking about these combinations, the presence of benefic Venus and benefic Rahu in the second house of the same horoscope or the presence of benefic Venus and benefic Sun in the second house of the same horoscope in the sign of Pisces can still get this female married with some delay, despite the presence of the already mentioned marriage delaying and marriage denying combinations in the horoscope of such female. The science of astrology is vast and there are billions of possible benefic as well as malefic combinations which can exist in different horoscopes and such combinations can change the results in a positive or in a negative way. Hence no conclusion should be drawn by looking at a single planet or even by looking at 3 or 4 planets in a horoscope as some other combinations may be present somewhere else in the same horoscope, which may change the results indicated by such planets.

Apart from delaying the marriage of the native under its influence, malefic retrograde Jupiter in the eighth house of a horoscope can also cause many problems in the marriage and married life of the native as such malefic influence may not only degrade the quality of marriage enjoyed by the native, but it may cause many problems in such marriage. Accordingly some natives under this malefic influence may have to suffer disturbances and problems of different type and different quantum through their marriages, depending on the type and strength of this malefic placement as well as depending on the overall tone of the horoscopes of these natives. For example, the presence of malefic retrograde Jupiter in the eighth house of a horoscope in the sign of Scorpio can cause problems in the married life of the native though such malefic placement may not cause much delay in his marriage.

The native under the malefic influence of such retrograde Jupiter in the eighth house of his horoscope may have to face issues related to lack of trust with her wife which means that there may not be much trust between the native and his wife and both of them may keep doubting each other, right from the start of their marriage. If malefic Mercury or malefic Rahu is placed in the seventh house of the same horoscope in the sign of Libra or if malefic Mars is present in the eighth house of the same horoscope in the sign of Scorpio along with malefic retrograde Jupiter, such problem of lack of trust between the native and his wife may intensify even more and accordingly they may suffer from serious issues which originate from lack of trust in each other.

It means that the native and his wife may keep suspecting each other in day to day life and they may not feel comfortable in each other's company. They may also argue a lot and such arguments may change into frequent fights with the passage of time. If there is no marriage saving combination present in the horoscope, the combined effect of such malefic retrograde Jupiter and other malefic planets mentioned in this example may eventually break the marriage of this native, after torturing him a lot.

In extreme cases, when a combination of malefic retrograde Jupiter and malefic Mars is present in the eighth house of a horoscope in the sign of Scorpio and malefic Mercury or malefic Rahu is placed in the seventh house of the same horoscope in the sign of Libra, the native under the combined effect of these malefic planets may have to face one or even more than one broken marriage, if there is no marriage saving combination present in the same horoscope. For example, the presence of a combination of benefic Venus and benefic Moon in the second house of the same horoscope in the sign of Taurus can still save the marriage of this native and the couple may finally be able to trust each other, after some initial years of serious lack of trust and problems in the marriage.

Apart from this, malefic retrograde Jupiter in the eight house of a horoscope can cause many other types of problems related to the marriage of the native and accordingly, different natives may suffer from these problems depending on their overall horoscopes. Malefic retrograde Jupiter in the eighth house of a horoscope can also cause problems related to the professional sphere of the native due to which, some natives under this malefic influence may have to face problems of different type and different intensity in their professional spheres, depending on the type and strength of this malefic influence, as well as depending on the overall tone of the horoscopes of these natives. Such malefic influence can also reduce the lifespan of the native and accordingly some natives suffering from this malefic influence may die at a relatively young or very young age by virtue of some disease, accident or even by virtue of a planned murder caused by such malefic retrograde Jupiter in the eighth house of their horoscopes.

Retrograde Jupiter in 9th House

Just like the eighth house, ninth house of a horoscope is also a very resourceful house and accordingly it carries great significance in defining the overall tone of a horoscope. Ninth house of a horoscope directly relates to the good karmas as well as bad karmas gathered by us, as well as those gathered by our ancestors and accordingly it can create a luck factor which is either good luck or bad luck for the native under its influence, depending on the good or bad karmas gathered by the native as well as his ancestors. Retrograde Jupiter placed in the ninth house of a horoscope can bless the native under its influence with good results in almost any sphere of his life including marriage, profession, children, education, fame and spiritual progress, if it is working positive in the horoscope. Accordingly, different natives benefitting from this benefic influence may witness good results where such good results can vary in type as well as in quantum depending on the type and strength of this benefic placement, as well as depending on the overall tone of the horoscopes of these natives.

Benefic retrograde Jupiter in the ninth house of a horoscope can bless the native with very good education, especially higher education and accordingly some native benefitting from this influence may receive education up to high, very high or even up to the highest levels, depending on their overall horoscopes. For example, the presence of benefic retrograde Jupiter in the ninth house of a horoscope in the sign of Libra can bless the native with special abilities like intelligence, good memory, good understanding and other such abilities. Accordingly the native under this benefic influence may perform well at studies right from the start and he may be known as a bright student right from his early age. If benefic Rahu or benefic Venus is placed in the fourth house of the same horoscope in the sign of Taurus, the benefits received by the native under the combined influence of these benefic planets may increase further and accordingly the native may perform even better at studies.

Such native may pursue his education to a high or very high level, under the combined effect of such benefic retrograde Jupiter in the ninth house of his horoscope and let's say benefic Rahu in the fourth house of his horoscope. It means that this native may specialize in some subject and he may obtain a degree of Masters in that subject or he may even achieve an academic degree of higher level, if the overall horoscope is supportive. For instance, the presence of benefic Sun or benefic Mercury in the fifth house of the same horoscope in the sign of Gemini can further improve this equation and accordingly the native under the combined effect of these benefic planets may pursue his education to the highest possible level, which means that he may earn a degree of doctorate in some subject or some other degree of the highest order relevant to a subject.

Benefic retrograde Jupiter in the ninth house of a horoscope can also bless the native with professional success and accordingly some natives under this benefic influence may achieve different type and different amount of professional success through different professional fields, depending on the type and strength of this benefic influence as well as depending on the overall tone of the horoscopes of these natives. Some natives under this benefic influence may become successful teachers after completing their studies on very high or even on the highest level in a subject and they may start teaching that subject. For example, the presence of benefic retrograde

Jupiter in the ninth house of a horoscope in the sign of Libra as mentioned in the previous example, can not only bless the native with top class education on a very high level, but such benefic influence can also bless the native with the profession of a successful teacher in the same subject.

Accordingly the native under the benefic influence of such positive retrograde Jupiter in the ninth house of his horoscope may become a teacher in a well reputed college or university, after completing his studies in some subject. If benefic Sun is present in the tenth house of the same horoscope in the sign of Scorpio, the native under the combined effect of such benefic retrograde Jupiter and benefic Sun may become a successful and well recognized teacher who may earn very good amount of respect among his students as well as among his colleagues by virtue of his very good grasp on the subject he teaches. If benefic Mars or benefic Mercury is also present in the ninth house of the same horoscope in the sign of Libra, the native under the combined influence of these benefic planets may also write books on the subject of his specialization. Such native may receive much appreciation and even some formal award for one or more than one of his book.

Benefic retrograde Jupiter in the ninth house of a horoscope can also render certain special abilities related to the fields of spiritualism, paranormal and other such fields, to the native under its influence. Accordingly some natives benefitting from this benefic placement may take interest in study and research related to the fields like spiritualism, astrology, numerology, religious studies and other such fields. If the overall horoscope of a native having such benefic influence in the ninth house of his horoscope is supportive, such native may make a career choice in one of these professions and he may achieve success and fame through one such field. For example, the presence of benefic retrograde Jupiter in the ninth house of a horoscope in the sign of Scorpio can make the native interested in faiths like astrology, meditation techniques for healing, yoga for healing physical as well as mental issues and other such faiths.

Hence the native under such benefic influence may engage in study and research related to one such faith or more than one such faith and he may take up such faith as a full time profession, if the overall horoscope of the native is supportive. For example, the presence of benefic Mercury in the eighth house of the same horoscope in the sign of Libra can improve this equation and the native under the combined effect of such benefic retrograde Jupiter and benefic Mercury may start practicing as an astrologer, a yoga teacher, a teacher who teaches meditation techniques or any other such type of teacher. Such native may achieve good amount of success, income, fame and recognition through his profession and he may keep achieving more and more with the passage of time. If benefic Rahu, benefic Moon or benefic Sun is placed in the first house of the same horoscope, the native under the combined effect of these benefic planets may achieve even more success and fame through such profession.

Looking at more possibilities in the same example, if benefic Mars is placed in the ninth house of the same horoscope in the sign of Scorpio, along with benefic retrograde Jupiter in the same house, the equation may improve further and the native may benefit even more. Such native under the combined effect of all these benefic planets may achieve success and fame on national level through one of these fields and he may also earn very good amount of money through his profession. The native under the combined effect of these benefic planets may also write some books on his subject and he may also appear on some television shows dealing with his subject of specialization. As more and more positive variables add to this equation, the native under the combined effect of such benefic retrograde Jupiter and other benefic planets in various houses of his horoscope may achieve even more success and fame through one such profession.

Some natives under this influence may take a slightly different path and they may choose to make a career choice in some field related to the study, practice and teaching of some religion or some religious faith and accordingly they may learn and preach the teachings of different religious faiths on different levels, depending on the type and strength of this benefic placement, as well as depending on the overall tone of the horoscopes of these natives. For example, the presence of benefic retrograde Jupiter in the ninth house of a horoscope in the sign of Taurus can motivate the native to choose a line of profession related to some type of practice belonging to some religion or some religious faith and accordingly such native may become a priest in some temple, a teacher in some religious institute or he may engage in some other type of practice related to some religious faith.

If benefic Moon is also present in the ninth house of the same horoscope in the sign of Taurus, the type of post achieved by this native and the quantum of success received by this native can increase many times. Accordingly, the native under the combined effect of such benefic retrograde Jupiter and benefic Moon in the ninth house of his horoscope in the sign of Taurus can become the head of a branch of some religious organization or he may become a head priest in some well established temple. Such native may possess a good amount of authority and many people may respect and follow him by virtue of such post of authority, as well as by virtue of the kind of knowledge and character possessed by him, due to the combined effect of these benefic planets. Since Moon is exalted in the sign of Taurus, the presence of benefic Moon along with benefic retrograde Jupiter in the sign of Taurus will not only enhance the working of Moon, but it will also provide extra strength to benefic retrograde Jupiter and accordingly, much better results may be witnessed by the native under such influences.

The presence of benefic Mercury in the fifth house of the same horoscope in the sign of Capricorn or in the eleventh house of the same horoscope in the sign of Cancer can further make this equation better and accordingly the native under the effect of these three benefic planets may achieve much more, through one such professional field. The native under the combined effect of such benefic retrograde Jupiter, benefic Moon and benefic Mercury may achieve even more success, fame and recognition and he may become the head of a very big branch of a religious organization or he may hold a post of high authority in the state body of a religious organization which operates on national or international level. If the overall horoscope of the native is supportive, he may even become the head of an entire state unit of a big religious organization or mission.

Let's now make a small change to this equation and see how the results can change. If benefic retrograde Jupiter is present in the ninth house of a horoscope in the sign of Taurus along with benefic Moon, and benefic Mercury is placed in the twelfth or eighth house of the same horoscope, say in the twelfth house of this horoscope in the sign of Leo, the field of profession chosen by the native may further change, though it may remain within the similar type of lines. The native under the combined effect of these benefic planets may follow the path of direct spiritualism and instead of practicing in some religious organization, he may get a post of high authority and responsibility in the state body of a spiritual organization, or he may even become the head of a spiritual organization.

Such native may have a good number of followers and he may himself achieve very good progress in the field of spiritualism. If benefic Rahu is present in the eighth house of the same horoscope in the sign of Aries or if it is present in the tenth house of the same horoscope in the sign of Gemini, the native under the combined effect of these benefic influences may start some spiritual mission or organization of his own. Such native may teach the techniques of meditation and other such techniques and methods which can help people achieve more and more spiritual growth. The combined effect of these benefic planets can render more and more success and fame to the native, and if benefic Venus is present in the eleventh house of the same horoscope in the sign of Cancer, the native may become a spiritual Guru of national fame and his fame may even spread to foreign countries also.

Benefic retrograde Jupiter in the ninth house of a horoscope can bless the native under its influence with good results in marriage also and accordingly some natives under this benefic influence may witness such good results where the type and quantum of these good results may vary from native to native depending on the type and strength of this benefic placement, as well as depending on the overall tone of the horoscope of a native in question. Some natives under this benefic influence may get married to someone hailing from a foreign country and they may get settled in that foreign country by virtue of their marriages. These natives may witness a good amount of rise in their standard of living as well as in their financial status after such settlement in a foreign country and they may also enjoy a very good marriage, provided their overall horoscope allows it.

For example, the presence of benefic retrograde Jupiter in the ninth house of a horoscope in the sign of Cancer can get the native married to someone belonging to a foreign country and accordingly the native under this benefic influence may get married to someone from a foreign country. If there are other benefic influences in the horoscope of this native, like if benefic Venus is placed in ninth, tenth, seventh or twelfth house of his horoscope, the native under the combined effect of these two benefic planets may get settled in that foreign country by virtue of his marriage. Such a combination of benefic retrograde Jupiter and benefic Venus can also bless the native with good professional results, good financial status, good overall results and a very good marriage. The fortune of such native may suddenly rise after his marriage and accordingly he may witness more and more good things happening to him after his marriage. As more positive planets add to this equation, the good results received by such native may increase in number as well as in quantum.

But all is not well with this placement of benefic retrograde Jupiter in the ninth house of a horoscope and such Jupiter can cause problems in almost every sphere of a native's life, if it turns malefic in a horoscope. Accordingly many natives under the malefic influence of this placement may have to witness bad results in many spheres of their lives including profession, marriage, children and overall well being, where the type and quantum of results received by different natives under this bad influence may be different depending on the type and strength of this malefic placement, as well as depending on the overall tone of the horoscopes of these natives. Professional sphere of the native is the first sphere which can be hit hard if malefic retrograde Jupiter is placed in the ninth house of a horoscope and accordingly some natives under this malefic influence may have to suffer on their professional fronts, in one way or the other.

These problems can increase in number as well as in quantum, if such malefic retrograde Jupiter placed in the ninth house of a horoscope forms Pitra Dosh in the horoscope. It should be noted that the mere presence of a malefic planet in the ninth house of a horoscope is not sufficient on its own to form Pitra Dosh in the horoscope, and it has to have certain minimum level of activity in order to form such Pitra Dosh and in order to actively do damages of higher levels. Moving on, if such malefic retrograde Jupiter forms Pitra dosh in the ninth house of horoscope, the native may feel the heat of this defect in many spheres of his life, depending on the type and strength of this placement as well as depending on the overall tone of his horoscope.

For example, Pitra Dosh formed by the presence of malefic retrograde Jupiter in the ninth house of a horoscope in the sign of Capricorn can trouble the native on the front of his profession as well as on the front of this marriage. Accordingly the native suffering from this defect may have to face problems when it comes to get good professional success and also when it comes to get married at proper time and enjoy a good marriage. However, this malefic placement is not capable of causing damages on a big scale as Jupiter is debilitated in the sign of Capricorn and accordingly the Pitra Dosh formed by such debilitated Jupiter may not be very strong and hence the problems caused by it may also be of low intensity. It means that though such native may experience delays when it comes to find a well paying job or a good profession, he may still be able to find one after some delay.

Similarly, the other problems faced by this native like low incomes from his profession and less overall professional growth may also bother him from time to time but even these problems are not likely to go beyond a certain point, as Pitra Dosh formed by such debilitated retrograde Jupiter is weak. However, if there are some other malefic planets present in the horoscope, which contribute to the malefic effect initiated by such Pitra Dosh, the equation can change and the native may have to suffer much more on the front of his profession. For example, the presence of malefic Rahu or malefic Ketu along with Saturn in almost any house of this horoscope can provide more strength to this defect and accordingly the native may have to struggle more in order to establish himself professionally and he may also have to suffer from many other problems in his professional sphere.

This is due to the fact that the affliction of malefic Rahu or Ketu to Saturn in this horoscope will reduce the strength of Saturn and since Saturn is the lord of the ninth house of this horoscope, double Pitra Dosh will be formed in the horoscope due to such affliction. The first Pitra Dosh is formed due to the malefic influence of negative retrograde Jupiter in the ninth house of this horoscope whereas the second Pitra Dosh is formed due to affliction of malefic Rahu or Ketu to Saturn in the horoscope, since any affliction to the planetary lord of ninth house in a horoscope also forms Pitra Dosh in that horoscope, according to the definition of this defect. Hence the native in this case will suffer from double Pitra Dosh and the combined effect of these malefic influences can make it even more difficult to achieve success through his profession.

Investigating this matter further, since Saturn is the lord of tenth house also in this horoscope, as the sign of Aquarius falls in the tenth house of this horoscope and Saturn is the planetary lord of Aquarius, the problem related to the professional sphere of the native may intensify even more. In this case, the lord of ninth house as well as the lord of tenth house of this horoscope is suffering from multiple afflictions through malefic retrograde Jupiter as well as through malefic Rahu or Ketu. Accordingly the native may find it very hard to even get a permanent profession as the house of profession which is the tenth house is afflicted and at the same time, the house of luck which is the ninth house is also afflicted. It means difficulty in finding a well paying or permanent profession due to afflicted lord of tenth house and it also means that even the luck factor of this native may not support him since the lord of ninth house of this horoscope is also afflicted by virtue of presence of malefic retrograde Jupiter in this house.

Hence the native may find it very hard to establish himself professionally and he may have to remain jobless many times in his life, for periods of some months or even for periods of some years, due to the combined effect of such malefic influences in his horoscope. If another malefic planet joins this combination, the problems of this native may further intensify, like the presence of malefic Sun in the sixth house of this horoscope in the sign of Libra can spell even more troubles for the native. The Sun is malefic, placed in sixth house and it is debilitated at the same time, which means even more troubles and accordingly the native may not be able to establish himself professionally, throughout his life, unless there are some really good combinations present in his horoscope which promote profession.

For instance, the presence of benefic Mercury in the tenth house of the same horoscope in the sign of Aquarius can still bless the native with a profession and if benefic Moon also joins benefic Mercury in the tenth house of this horoscope, the equation may improve even further. Such native may have to lose his job many times due to the combined effect of such malefic planets, but he may find another job soon after losing one job, due to the combined effect of such benefic Mercury and benefic Moon in the tenth house of his horoscope. If benefic Venus is placed in the fourth house of this horoscope, in the sign of Leo, the equation may become even better and accordingly the native may face even fewer problems in his professional sphere. It should be noted that the net luck of a native and the possibility of anything good or bad happening to a native is the resultant of the interaction of so many good as well as bad influences in his horoscope, and as more and more such influences change, the net luck factor of the native also changes, which means different results can be experienced by the native.

Retrograde Jupiter in 10th House

When working positively, retrograde Jupiter in the tenth house of a horoscope can bless the native with many good things including good results related to profession, marriage, fame, spiritualism and education. Accordingly different natives benefitting from this positive influence may experience good results of different type and different quantum depending on the type and strength of this placement, as well as depending on the overall tone of the horoscopes of these natives. Benefic retrograde Jupiter in the tenth house of a horoscope can render professional success to the native under its influence through a great number of professional fields since tenth house of a horoscope primarily deals with the professional aspect of the native and accordingly, the placement of any benefic planet in this house of the horoscope is likely to bring good results related to the professional sphere of the native.

This placement of benefic retrograde Jupiter in tenth house of a horoscope is a good placement when it comes to render creative abilities to the native and accordingly some natives benefitting from this placement may be gifted with different types of creative abilities depending on their overall horoscopes. Some of these natives may have special talents like singing, writing, directing, acting, dancing, painting and other such talents and accordingly they may achieve different amounts of success through such talents, depending on their overall horoscopes. For example, the presence of benefic retrograde Jupiter in the tenth house of a horoscope in the sign of Gemini can bless the native under its influence with special abilities related to the fields of fashion modeling, acting, singing, writing and other such abilities.

As a result, the native may become interested in making a career in one of these fields through this benefic influence on its own may not be sufficient to bless the native with a successful career in one of these fields and it may need support from other positive influences in the horoscope. If benefic Moon is also present in the tenth house of the same horoscope, the native under the combined effect of such benefic retrograde Jupiter and benefic Moon in the tenth house of his horoscope in the sign of Gemini can see better results related to one of these professions. Such native may either become a fashion model or an actor, or he may first work as a model and then he may switch to the field of acting, though even the combination of these two benefic planets may not be able to render very good amount of professional success to the native through one of these fields and more positive influences may be needed in the horoscope.

Moving on with the same example, if benefic Venus, benefic Rahu or benefic Mercury is placed in the eleventh house of the same horoscope in the sign of Cancer, the native under the combined effect of such benefic retrograde Jupiter and Moon in the tenth house of his horoscope and one benefic planet say Mercury in the eleventh house of his horoscope may witness even better results. Such native may achieve good amount of success and fame as a lead actor in some television programs or he may also perform as a lead actor in some movies though he may still not become a very famous movie star, despite the presence of such benefic combinations, and he may need more positive influences.

The presence of benefic Rahu in tenth house of the same horoscope in the sign of Gemini or in the eleventh house of this horoscope in the sign of Cancer may just do the needful and accordingly the native under the combined effect of benefic retrograde Jupiter in tenth house of his horoscope and other benefic planets mentioned in this example may achieve very good amount of success as a lead movie actor. Such native may earn very good amount of money and fame as an actor and he may have a big number of fans who like and follow him. If benefic Venus is present in the first, fifth, ninth, tenth or eleventh house of the same horoscope, the native under the combined effect of all these benefic planets may achieve phenomenal success as a lead actor. Such native may not only remain an actor and he may achieve the title of a real star or even that of a superstar, if the rest of his horoscope is supportive.

Some other natives under this benefic influence may become writers or singers who may write or sing on different themes and who may earn money and fame through one of these professions. For example, the presence of benefic retrograde Jupiter in the tenth house of a horoscope in the sign of Gemini can also render good writing abilities to the native under its influence and if there are some other factors present in his horoscope which support a career as a writer, the native may become a professional writer. For instance, if benefic Mars or benefic Mercury is also present in the tenth house of the same horoscope, the native under the combined influence of these benefic planets may possess very good writing abilities and accordingly he may become a professional writer who may write songs, movie scripts or even books, depending on the overall theme of his horoscope.

It is interesting to note that though benefic retrograde Jupiter is present in the tenth house of a horoscope in the sign of Gemini in both the examples, the presence of other benefic influences with such retrograde Jupiter as well as in other houses of the same horoscope can make this native a professional actor, a professional writer or even a professional singer. This is why the overall theme of a horoscope must be checked properly before making a prediction on the basis of one or two planets in the horoscope. Moving on with the example, the native under the combined influence of such benefic retrograde Jupiter and Mercury in the tenth house of his horoscope in the sign of Gemini may become a professional writer and he may achieve good amount of success through this talent.

If benefic Venus or benefic Rahu is placed in the third house of the same horoscope in the sign of Scorpio, the equation may become even more favorable and accordingly the native blessed by the combined effect of these benefic planets may achieve even more success and fame as a writer. Such native may not only write for movies or songs, he may also writer books on various topics and he may also receive good amount of recognition and appreciation through such books. If the overall horoscope of the native is supportive, he may even receive some formal award for one of his books. For example, the presence of benefic Moon in the tenth house of the same horoscope in the sign of Gemini can do this trick and accordingly the native under the combined effect of such benefic retrograde Jupiter and other benefic planets may receive one or more than one award for some of his writings.

Considering the third possibility under the same example, the presence of benefic retrograde Jupiter in the tenth house of a horoscope in the sign of Gemini can also bless the native with good abilities related to the field of singing and accordingly the native under such benefic influence may be interested in singing also. However this benefic placement on its own is not capable of rendering very good singing talent to the native under its influence in most cases, and more support from the horoscope of such native may be required. If benefic Moon, benefic Rahu or benefic Mercury is placed in the second house of the same horoscope in the sing of Libra, the native may just get blessed with sufficient amount of singing talent to become a professional singer. Hence the native under the combined effect of such benefic retrograde Jupiter in the tenth house of his horoscope and one more benefic planet say benefic Rahu in the second house of his horoscope in the sign of Libra may become a professional singer though these two planets may still not be capable of blessing the native with good amount of success as a singer and more positive influences may be needed.

If benefic Venus is present in the eleventh house of the same horoscope in the sign of Cancer, the horoscope may become even better and accordingly the results may improve. The native under the combined effect of such benefic retrograde Jupiter, benefic Rahu and benefic Venus in the already mentioned houses of his horoscope may become a successful singer. Such native may earn good amount of money and fame through his singing talent and he may also sing as a playback singer for many famous stars of his time. If benefic Moon is present in the eleventh or second house of the same horoscope, the native under the combined influence of all these benefic planets may achieve even more success as a singer and he may have a big fan following.

Moving on, if benefic Mercury is also present in the tenth house of the horoscope in the sign of Gemini or it is present in the first house of the same horoscope in the sign of Virgo, the equation may improve further and the native may now become even more successful. Such native may become a very famous singer, not only in his country, but in some foreign countries also and he may even receive formal awards for his singing on national or even on international level, provided his overall horoscope supports it. You see how the results achieved by the same native change when some variables are changed in the horoscope like in this example where benefic retrograde Jupiter placed in tenth house of a horoscope in the sign of Gemini can make the native a professional actor, writer or singer, depending on the overall tone of his horoscope.

Some natives under this benefic influence may also achieve a post of power and authority in some government department as such benefic placement is fully capable of rendering such results to the native. Accordingly some natives under this benefic influence may work for government in different departments as well as on different posts, depending on the type and strength of this benefic influence, as well as depending on their overall horoscopes. For example, the presence of benefic retrograde Jupiter in the tenth house of a horoscope in the sign of Sagittarius can bless the native with a job with government and accordingly such native may become a teacher, a banker, a police officer, an administrative officer or a revenue officer, depending on the overall tone of his horoscope.

Following the last case, the presence of benefic retrograde Jupiter in the tenth house of a horoscope can bless the native with the post of a revenue officer of some type, if there are other supporting influences present in the horoscope of such native. For instance, if benefic Venus in present in the first house of this horoscope in the sign of Pisces when benefic retrograde Jupiter is placed in the tent house of the same horoscope, the native under the combined effect of these benefic influences may become an officer with income tax department or with some other revenue department of the government. If benefic Mars is present in the second house of the same horoscope in the sign of Aries, the native under the combined influence of these benefic planets may directly get appointed as a high class officer in some revenue department of government and he may witness good amount of success and progress in his career. As more positive planets keep adding to the horoscope of this native, he may achieve even more success through his profession.

On the other hand, retrograde Jupiter in the tenth house of a horoscope can become a difficult to handle placement of this planet, if it goes negative in the horoscope. Malefic retrograde Jupiter in tenth house of a horoscope can trouble the native with problems related to profession, marriage, health, overall well being, reputation, status and many other things. Accordingly some natives suffering from this bad influence may have to face problems which may be of different type and different quantum, depending on the type and strength of this placement as well as depending on the overall tone of the horoscopes of these natives. As tenth house of a horoscope primarily represents the professional aspect of a native, the native under this malefic influence are likely to feel the maximum heat of this bad influence, in the sphere of their professions.

Some natives under such malefic influence may not be able to settle in any type of professional field till late or very late in their lives depending on their overall horoscopes, and these natives may have to keep changing job after job or profession after profession under the malefic influence of this placement. Some other natives under this bad impact may not be able to get a profession at all till late or very late in their lives and they may have to wait long, even in order to start. Yet some other natives under this malefic influence may have to face financial losses, setbacks, legal issues, bad reputation and other such problems through their fields of profession. For example, the presence of malefic retrograde Jupiter in the tenth house of a horoscope in the sign of Taurus can not only delay the professional settlement of the native, but it can also cause many disturbances in his profession, as and when he gets one.

Accordingly the native suffering from such bad influence may not get a job suitable according to his academic qualifications or according to some other qualifications that he may have, and such native may have to settle for a job which is below his standards. If malefic Ketu or malefic Saturn is also present in the tenth house of the same horoscope, the native under the combined effect of such malefic retrograde Jupiter and one more malefic planet let's say Saturn in the tenth house of his horoscope in the sign of Taurus, may have to face even more problems through his professional sphere. Such native may not only have to accept jobs which are below or far below his standards many times in his life, but he may also have to remain jobless many times in his life and such periods of being jobless can vary in length, depending on the other factors in his horoscope.

It means that such native may not get a job suitable according to his abilities or qualifications and he may have to settle for a low standard job. The native may not like this job much and he may keep looking for some better job and once he finds a better one, he may quit the first one, only to come across even worse things in the second one and then he may have to quit that one also, or he may get fired from such job. Then the native under the combined effect of such malefic retrograde Jupiter and malefic Saturn in the tenth house of his horoscope may have to remain jobless for some time, before he is able to find another job, which is once again not up to his standards. If malefic Venus is present in the eighth house of the same horoscope or if malefic Ketu is present in the eleventh house of this horoscope, the native under the combined effect of these malefic planets may have to remain jobless for long periods of time like for a year or even more, more than once in his life.

Such native may find a job below his standards, get out of it after some time due to various reasons, remain jobless for some time, then find another job below his standards and then once again get out of it. This process may keep repeating and the native under the combined malefic effect of such retrograde Jupiter, Saturn and Ketu may fall prey to this vicious circle throughout his life, if there are no other profession promoting benefic combinations in his horoscope. For example, the presence of a combination of benefic Sun and benefic Mercury in the first house of the same horoscope in the sign of Leo may improve this equation and accordingly the native may suffer much less on his professional front.

If benefic Mars is present in the fourth house of the same horoscope in the sign of Scorpio, this equation may change altogether and the native may even witness the results which are opposite in nature to the previous results. Such native under the combined influence of all these malefic and benefic planets may get selected for a permanent job in some government department which deals with defense like police force or which deals with administration, and he may earn good amount of money, success and authority through such job. It should be noted that a horoscope is all about its overall tone and no conclusions should be drawn from one or two planets in horoscope. As you can see that in this example, even a malefic combination of malefic retrograde Jupiter and malefic Saturn can work in favor of native, if there are some other such benefic combinations in the horoscope of the native, which can channelize even the negative energy generated by such malefic planets, in a positive way.

Malefic retrograde Jupiter in the tenth house of a horoscope can also render criminal tendencies to some natives under it influence and accordingly some natives under such malefic influence may pursue a life of crime and they may have to face many bad results through such life of crime. For example, the presence of malefic retrograde Jupiter in the tenth house of a horoscope in the sign of Aquarius can render criminal tendencies to the native and accordingly such native may take much interest in crime and criminal activities though he may not actively start engaging in crimes as such malefic influence alone may not be sufficient to make the native an active criminal.

However, if malefic Rahu is present in the eleventh house of the same horoscope in the sign of Pisces or it is present in the first house of the same horoscope in the sign of Taurus, or it is present in the sixth house of the same horoscope in the sign of Libra, the equation may change considerably. The native under the combined effect of such malefic retrograde Jupiter in tenth house of his horoscope and malefic Rahu in one of the already mentioned houses, say in the first house of his horoscope, may actively engage in a life of crime and he may become a criminal. Such native may start engaging in various types of crimes from an early age and he is likely to work with or work for an organized criminal network such as a mafia group of some type.

If malefic Moon, malefic Sun or malefic Venus is present in the sixth house of the same horoscope in the sign of Libra, the problem may intensify even more. The presence of one of these planets say malefic Moon in the sixth house of this horoscope in the sign of Libra can develop even stronger criminal tendencies in the native and accordingly the native may engage in crimes of bigger level and bigger quantum. Such native under the combined effect of such malefic retrograde Jupiter and other malefic planets in various houses of his horoscope may have to face disgrace, court cases, physical injuries and prison sentences by virtue of his engagement in various types of crimes.

If malefic Saturn or malefic Venus is placed in the twelfth house of the same horoscope in the sign of Aries or if one of them is present in the eighth house of the same horoscope in the sign of Sagittarius, the native under the combined effect of these malefic planets may have to spend many years of his life or a big part of his life in prison by virtue of a crime committed by him. If there are no other grace saving combinations in the horoscope of this native, he may even have to face a life sentence or even a capital punishment for one of the crimes committed by him.

Retrograde Jupiter in 11th House

When benefic in nature, retrograde Jupiter placed in the eleventh house of a horoscope can bless the native with good results related to profession, overall financial status, marriage, health and many other aspects of his life. Accordingly the natives under the effect of this benefic influence may experience good results which can be different in type and quantum depending on the type and strength of this placement, as well as depending on the overall tone of the horoscopes of these natives. Benefic retrograde Jupiter in eleventh house of a horoscope is one of the best placements of this planet when it comes to bless the native with professional success and financial benefits, as such benefic influence can not only render good amount of professional success to the native under its influence, but it can also make the native grow more and more with the passage of time.

Some natives under this benefic influence may become interested in the study and practice of specific fields related to financial markets like stock markets, capital funds, venture funding and other such fields which are different branches of financial field but which are not direct financial institutes like banks. For example, the presence of benefic retrograde Jupiter in the eleventh house of a horoscope in the sign of Pisces can make the native interested in one of these lines like the practice of stock market and accordingly the native may plan for engaging in one such line on professional basis. However, this benefic placement alone may not be sufficient to generate such results and it may need support from other positive influences in the horoscope of the native, in order to convert this interest into full time profession.

The presence of benefic Mercury in the first house of the same horoscope in the sign of Taurus can improve this equation and accordingly the native under the combined influence of such benefic retrograde Jupiter and benefic Mercury may engage in one such financial line, on professional basis. Such native may engage in the practice of stock markets and he may either make profits by investing his own money or he may manage stock market investment profiles of his clients, by operating through a stock market investment consultant company. If benefic Saturn is placed in eleventh house of this horoscope in the sign of Pisces along with benefic retrograde Jupiter, the native under the combined effect of these three planets may make his own investments in stock markets and he may earn good amount of profits through such investments, from time to time, depending on the overall tone of his horoscope.

However if benefic Rahu is placed in the sixth house of this horoscope in the sign of Libra and benefic retrograde Jupiter is alone in the eleventh house of this horoscope when benefic Mercury is present in the first house of the same horoscope, the native under the combined effect of these benefic planets may open a company which manages the investment profiles of various clients who want to invest in stock markets and who want to make profits through such investments. If benefic Venus also joins benefic Rahu in sixth house of this horoscope in the sign of Libra, the overall equation may improve and as a result, the native under the combined effect of all these benefic planets may achieve much more success through one such profession.

Such native may become the owner of a company which provides guidance for financial investments and which also manages such financial investments on behalf of their clients, and such company may not only fetch very good financial incomes to the native, but it may also keep expanding with time. It means that such company may have multiple branches which may keep opening in one city after the other, with the passage of time, if the overall horoscope is supportive. The presence of benefic Moon in the first house of the same horoscope in the sign of Taurus along with benefic Mercury or the presence of benefic Moon in the eleventh house of the same horoscope in the sign of Pisces along with benefic retrograde Jupiter can further increase the amount of success received by the native. Accordingly, the native under the combined influence of these benefic planets may achieve even more success and growth through one such profession.

Benefic retrograde Jupiter in the eleventh house of a horoscope can also bless the native with good, very good or great amount of success through some other businesses also, and accordingly some natives under this good influence may earn money through various businesses, where the amount of money earned and the type of business practiced by such natives may be different depending on the type and strength of this benefic placement, as well as depending on the overall tone of the horoscopes of these natives. For example, the presence of benefic retrograde Jupiter in the eleventh house of a horoscope in the sign of Aquarius can bless the native with success through some social media setup or through any other type of business which deals with people or networking of some type.

Accordingly the native under this benefic influence may work for some social media company or for some other type of company that deals in networking of some type, like a web hosting company, an internet services providing company, some telephonic services providing company or some other company of this type. This native may engage in a job instead of his own business, as such benefic retrograde Jupiter alone in eleventh house of a horoscope is not capable of blessing the native with his own business and it may need support from other positive influences in the same horoscope. The presence of benefic Moon, benefic Venus, benefic Saturn, benefic Mars or benefic Rahu in the eleventh house may provide the required support and accordingly, the native under the combined influences of these two benefic planets in the eleventh house of his horoscope, say benefic retrograde Jupiter and benefic Rahu in the eleventh house of his horoscope in the sign of Aquarius may witness better results.

Hence the native may either get a post of authority in one such company where he receives very good salary and other benefits also, or he may start his own business related to one of these fields and he may make good amount of money through such business. The native may start a showroom which provides products and services related to one of these services like telephone or mobile services or devices, internet related services or devices, satellite television related products or services, or any other such type of services and products. If benefic Moon, benefic Saturn, benefic Venus or benefic Mercury is placed in the third house of the same horoscope in the sign of Cancer, the native under the combined influence of such benefic retrograde Jupiter and other benefic planets may achieve even more success through one such business.

The native may witness very good growth and income through his business and he may become the exclusive franchise of one of such products or services, for a specific region. If from the already mentioned planets, benefic Mercury is present in the third house of this horoscope in the sign of Cancer and benefic Moon is placed in the first house of this horoscope in the sign of Taurus, this equation can improve even more. The placement of such benefic Moon in the first house of this horoscope can especially prove very beneficial as such Moon is not only benefic, but it is also exalted and placed in the first house of the horoscope. Such placement will not only add to the benefic effects indicated by benefic retrograde Jupiter and benefic Rahu in the eleventh house of the horoscope, but it will also enhance the positive results indicated by benefic Mercury placed in the third house of this horoscope.

This is due to the fact that Mercury is placed in the sign of Cancer and the presence of benefic Moon in its sign of exaltation in the first house of this horoscope will provide strength to all the benefic planets in this horoscope, with maximum strength being provided to benefic Mercury as it is placed in the sign directly ruled by the Moon. Accordingly, the native benefitting from the combined effect of all these planets may not only achieve very good amount of success through one such business, he may also start a company of his own, which provides products and services related to one of the fields already mentioned in this example. Such company may expand on state as well as on national level, as more and more positive and supportive influences keep adding to the horoscope of this native.

Some other natives benefitting from this benefic influence may venture into the fields which deal with the manufacturing, marketing or selling of clothes, fashion accessories, artificial jewelry items, hotel business, airline business, the field of information and technology, software industry, teaching and coaching institutions and many other lines. Accordingly different natives under the effect of such benefic retrograde Jupiter may deal in different professional spheres and they may achieve different amount of success through such fields, depending on the type and strength of this benefic influence, as well as depending on the overall tone of their horoscopes. For example, the presence of benefic retrograde Jupiter in the eleventh house of a horoscope in the sign of Libra can motivate the native to pursue a career related to the field of airlines.

If benefic Venus or benefic Rahu is placed in the second house of the same horoscope in the sign of Capricorn, the native under the combined effect of such benefic retrograde Jupiter and one other such planet say benefic Venus may engage in some type of job related to the airline industry. The presence of such a benefic combination in the horoscope of a female can make her an air hostess whereas the presence of such benefic combination in the horoscope of a male can either make him an air host or it can make him hold a post in an airline, where he deals with the boarding of the passengers in that airline. However, if benefic Rahu or benefic Mars is placed in the first house of this horoscope in the sign of Sagittarius and benefic Venus is placed in twelfth house of the same horoscope in the sign of Scorpio, the combined effect of these benefic planets may instead make the native become a pilot. Accordingly, the native may become a pilot in some airline or he may engage in some other similar type of job in an airline company.

Benefic retrograde Jupiter in the eleventh house of a horoscope can also give good results related to marriage and married life of the native and accordingly some natives under this benefic influence may witness different types of benefic results related to the sphere of their marriage, depending on the type and strength of this benefic influence, as well as depending on the overall tone of their horoscopes. For example, benefic retrograde Jupiter in the eleventh house of a horoscope in the sign of Cancer can bless the native with a devoted and caring partner. Accordingly the male native benefitting from such influence may get a wife who is caring, attentive and devoted to him and who may add much value to his life, whereas a female native under this benefic influence may get a husband who is rich and established and who at the same time takes good care of her needs.

Such female may witness good amount of rise in her financial as well as in her social status, by virtue of her marriage to such rich and established man. If the overall horoscope of this female is supportive, she may enjoy very good benefits and authority through her marriage as well as through her husband. For instance, if benefic Mercury is present in the seventh house of the same horoscope in the sign of Pisces along with benefic Moon, benefic Rahu or benefic Venus, such female native may not only get a rich and well established husband, but she may also have a commanding position in her marriage. It means that the husband of such female may take very good care of her, he may take her advice in every important matter and he may fulfill most of her wishes.

On the other hand, retrograde Jupiter placed in the eleventh house of a horoscope can cause many problems in many spheres of the life of the native under its influence, if it turns negative in the horoscope. Accordingly, different natives suffering from this malefic influence may have to come across many problems in different spheres of their lives, depending on the type and strength of this placement as well as depending on the overall horoscopes of such natives. Malefic retrograde Jupiter in the eighth house of a horoscope can especially prove very bad for professional as well as financial aspect of the native under its influence due to which such native may feel the heat of this bad influence in these spheres. For example, the presence of malefic retrograde Jupiter in the eleventh house of a horoscope in the sign of Leo can cause problems related to the professional as well as financial sphere of the native.

Accordingly such native may not be able to find well paying jobs and he may have to work for jobs which are not paying him according to his qualifications or according to the market standard salaries for such jobs. The presence of malefic Rahu, malefic Ketu, malefic Venus or some other malefic planet in the same house of the horoscope along with malefic retrograde Jupiter can further complicate the matters and as a result, the native under the combined effect of these malefic planets say malefic retrograde Jupiter and malefic Ketu in the eleventh house of his horoscope in the sign of Leo may have to suffer even more.

Such native may have to remain jobless for long periods of time more than once in his life and in order to get out of his status of being jobless; he may have to accept jobs which are not paying him according to his standards or according to the market standards for such jobs. It means that though he market standard salary for a job may be an amount of 5000 per month in his local currency, he may have to accept the same job for 4000 or even less, as the employer may take undue advantage of his dire need for that job. Hence the employer may refuse to pay according to market standards and the native may have to compromise on low salary, in order to start earning something.

Some other natives under this malefic influence may face financial problems which may come due to unwanted expenses, bad habits like gambling, or which may come through some of their friends and accordingly some natives under this bad influence may have to face financial problems of various kinds depending on the type and strength of this malefic placement, as well as depending on their overall horoscopes. For example, the presence of malefic retrograde Jupiter in the eleventh house of a horoscope in the sign of Taurus may trouble the native with financial losses which may come due to unwanted expenses like they may have to spend money towards the treatment of diseases from time to time. Such malefic influence can also trouble the native with financial losses through his friends which means that the native under the malefic influence of such retrograde Jupiter may lend some money to some of his friends from time to time when they are in need, but such money may almost never come back to the native and he may have to face financial tightness due to this.

The presence of malefic Rahu, malefic Ketu or malefic Saturn in the eleventh house of a horoscope in the sign of Taurus along with malefic retrograde Jupiter can further intensify this problem. Accordingly, the native under the combined effect of these malefic planets may not only have to suffer financial losses by virtue of his friends borrowing money from him and then not returning it, but he may also have to lose some of his very good friends in the process. It means that the native may lend a handsome amount of money to one of his close friends in the time of his need and such friend may keep making excuses for a long period of time when the native asks him to return his money. The native may try his best to get his money back from this friend, who may be even capable of returning such money, but he may not return his money, and in the process, their friendship may come to an end, with the money still not returned to the native.

If there are some other specific negative indicators in the horoscope of this native, the native may not only lose some of his friends, but such friends may turn his enemies for a long period of time or even for life. For example, the presence of malefic Mercury, malefic Mars or malefic Venus in the sixth house of the same horoscope in the sign of Sagittarius can intensify the problems suffered by native in the same example. Accordingly, the native under the combined influence of such malefic retrograde Jupiter and other malefic planets may have to experience some of his friends turn enemies towards him due to various reasons. Such friends can trouble the native a lot and they may even plan a serious conspiracy against the native, if there are more negative influences in his horoscope and the overall horoscope is also not supportive.

Retrograde Jupiter in 12th House

When benefic in nature, retrograde Jupiter placed in twelfth house of a horoscope can bless the native with good results related to the sphere of profession, marriage, finances, overall health and well being, spiritualism and many other spheres of his life. Accordingly different natives under the impact of this benefic influence may witness good results of different type and different quantum depending on the type and strength of this placement in their horoscopes, as well as depending on overall tone of their horoscopes. Such benefic influence in the twelfth house of a horoscope can bless the native with special abilities related to various creative fields like acting, singing, writing, painting, sculpting, designing of various types and many other such creative abilities. Accordingly some natives under this benefic influence may adopt some creative field as their field of profession and they may earn good or very good amount of money and success through such creative field.

For example, the presence of benefic retrograde Jupiter in the twelfth house of a horoscope in the sign of Libra can bless the native with creative abilities like writing, acting and other such abilities and accordingly the native may take much interest in some of these activities though this placement alone may not be capable of making him engage in one of these creative fields on professional basis and it may need more support from the horoscope. If benefic Saturn is placed is also placed in the twelfth house of the same horoscope in the sign of Libra or if benefic Saturn is placed in the eleventh house of the same horoscope in the sign of Virgo, this equation may become stronger and the results may change. The native under the combined influence of such benefic retrograde Jupiter and benefic Saturn may become good at the creative ability of writing on various topics though such benefic combination may promote other types of creative abilities also.

Hence the native may become more and more interested in writing on different topics or in some other activities related to writing and he may engage in writing or other activities related to writing on professional basis. The other activities mentioned here mean the activities like copy editing of a book or some other type of writing where the native is directly not writing something of his own, but he is trying to improve the quality of an already finished writing, which is a creative ability on its own. Such native under the combined effect of these two benefic planets may make decent amount of money through such profession, though the combination of these two planets on their own may not be sufficient to bless the native with very good amount of success through such writing abilities.

If benefic Mercury is placed in tenth or eleventh house of the same horoscope, the equation may improve further and accordingly, the native under the combined effect of these benefic planets may achieve more success through such profession related to writing. The presence of benefic retrograde Jupiter in twelfth house of this horoscope in the sign of Libra and a combination of benefic Saturn and benefic Mercury in the eleventh house of this horoscope in the sign of Virgo can prove a powerful combination and it can bless the native with very good amount of success through such creative profession. The presence of benefic Moon or benefic Rahu in eleventh or twelfth house of the same horoscope can further improve this equation and accordingly the native under the combined influence of all these benefic planets may not only write books on various topics, he may earn very good amount of success, money and fame through his writings.

Taking another example, the presence of benefic retrograde Jupiter in the twelfth house of a horoscope in the sign of Cancer can make the native more interested in acting, than in writing and accordingly, the native under such benefic influence may take interest in acting on various levels. Such native may perform in some shows or programs during his school years and he may carry this interest forward, if there are other benefic and supporting influences in his horoscope. For instance, the presence of benefic Mercury in the eleventh house of the same horoscope in the sign of Gemini can increase this talent much more in the native and accordingly the native may pursue the line of acting as his active profession. Though the combined effect of these two planets can make the native pursue a career in acting, this combination may not be sufficient to bless the native with required success and it may need more support from his horoscope.

If there is no such support present in the horoscope of this native, he may become a movie or television actor, but he may not achieve much success through such profession and he may have to keep struggling for a long period of time, in order to find and benefit from the right type of opportunities in this field. However if benefic Sun or benefic Rahu is also present in the eleventh house of this horoscope, the combined effect of such benefic Mercury and let's say benefic Rahu in the eleventh house of this horoscope in the sign of Gemini, along with benefic retrograde Jupiter in the twelfth house of the same horoscope in the sign of Cancer can improve this situation a lot.

Accordingly the native under the combined influence of these benefic planets may not only become a professional actor, but he may also achieve good amount of success and fame through such acting. The presence of benefic Moon or benefic Venus in the tenth house of this horoscope can further improve this equation and the native under the combined effect of all these benefic planets may witness very good amount of success and fame as a lead actor in movies, provided his overall horoscope is supportive. Such native may also have a good number of people following him as fans and he may also achieve some formal award or even more than one award for some piece of his acting. As more and more positive planets keep adding to the equation, the success achieved by this native may increase even more.

The presence of benefic retrograde Jupiter in the twelfth house of a horoscope can also create spiritual or other similar tendencies in the native and accordingly some natives under such benefic influence may have good interest in one or more than one such field like spiritualism, paranormal or other such field. Such interests of the native may change by margins as the type and strength of this benefic influence in the twelfth house of a horoscope changes. For example, the presence of benefic retrograde Jupiter in the twelfth house of a horoscope in the sign of Pisces or Cancer may bend the native more towards the direct path of spiritualism if the overall horoscope of the native under consideration allows it.

On the other hand, the presence of benefic retrograde Jupiter in the twelfth house of a horoscope in the sign of Scorpio or Virgo may bend the native more towards faiths like astrology, numerology and other such healing faiths. Similarly, the presence of benefic retrograde Jupiter in the twelfth house of a horoscope in the sign of Sagittarius or Leo can motivate the native to follow the path of studying and teaching meditation techniques which are primarily not meant for direct connection with the supreme soul, but which are primarily meant for having a better and more able body and mind. All these possibilities can further change by small or even by big percentages in all these three examples, depending on the overall tone of the horoscope of the native in question.

Moving on with the second example among these three, the presence of benefic retrograde Jupiter in the twelfth house of a horoscope in the sign of Scorpio can motivate the native towards the study of some faith like astrology and accordingly the native may study various writings related to one such faith, let's say astrology. If benefic Moon is present in the first house of this horoscope in the sign of Sagittarius, the native under the combined effect of such benefic retrograde Jupiter and benefic Moon in the twelfth and first house of his horoscope respectively, may not only read books or other such content on astrology, but he may also conduct deep study or even research in this field. Such native may even start practicing as an amateur astrologer after conducting studies and researches up to a point, and he may even become a professional astrologer, if there are some other benefic influences in his horoscope which support this fact.

If benefic Mercury or benefic Rahu is present in the tenth house of this horoscope in the sign of Virgo, the native under the combined effect of such benefic retrograde Jupiter, Moon and one more benefic planet let's say Rahu in the already mentioned houses of his horoscope may become a professional astrologer and he may earn good amount of success and money through this profession. If a combination of benefic Rahu and benefic Mercury is placed in the tenth house of this horoscope in the sign of Virgo, the native may achieve even more success and he may become a famous astrologer. Such native is likely to achieve more fame and success compared to the amount of money earned by him, which means that this native may not be earning as much money, as other astrologers of his fame may earn. It is usually due to the reason that such native may not be primarily interested in money and he may be primarily interested in success, fame and more knowledge about this profession.

This situation can change altogether if this combination of benefic Mercury and benefic Rahu is placed in the eleventh house of this horoscope in the sign of Libra, instead of being present in the tenth house of this horoscope in the sign of Virgo. In this case, the native under the combined effect of such benefic retrograde Jupiter, benefic Moon, benefic Mercury and benefic Rahu in the already mentioned houses of his horoscope may enter into this profession with the aim of earning money and fame, and accordingly he may become a more famous and rich astrologer, than a more successful or expert astrologer.

It should be noted that a famous astrologer may be the one who advertises a lot through various platforms and accordingly he becomes more known, though he may not possess very good amount of knowledge and expertise on his subject. On the other hand, an expert and successful astrologer is the one who has very good accuracy in his readings and who has a big percentage of satisfied clients who have seen very good results through him. Hence, even small variations in the theme of a horoscope can make big changes in the final outcome as astrology is a science of permutations and combinations and any change of any type is always important, and hence it should be studied carefully.

Apart from this, benefic retrograde Jupiter in the twelfth house of a horoscope can bless the native under its influence with many other good results related to many spheres of his life including profession and marriage. Such results can be different in case of different natives benefitting from this good influence depending on the type and strength of this placement, as well as depending on the overall tone of the horoscopes of these natives. On the other hand, malefic retrograde Jupiter in the twelfth house of a horoscope can cause many problems and troubles in many spheres of the life of the native under its influence and accordingly such native may feel the heat of this bad influence in the sphere of his marriage, profession, health, financial equation or in some other sphere of his life, depending on his overall horoscope.

Malefic retrograde Jupiter in the twelfth house of a horoscope can cause many types of problems in the marriage and married life of the native under its influence and accordingly different natives suffering from this bad impact may have to face problems related to their marriages, which are different in type and intensity, depending on the type and strength of this bad influence as well as depending on the overall tone of the horoscopes of these natives. Some natives under this malefic influence may not be able to get married at proper ages and they may have to wait till late or very late in their lives in order to get married, whereas some other natives suffering from this malefic placement may have to suffer disturbances through their marriages. For example, the presence of benefic retrograde Jupiter in the twelfth house of a horoscope in the sign of Libra can delay the marriage of the native and accordingly such native may not get married till late in his life.

If malefic Rahu or malefic Mars is placed in the fifth house of this horoscope in the sign of Pisces, the native under the combined influence of these malefic planets may engage in a love affair with someone and such relationship of this native may continue for many years. However the combined influence of such malefic retrograde Jupiter in the twelfth house of this horoscope in the sign of Libra and let's say malefic Rahu in the fifth house of the same horoscope in the sign of Pisces, may not let this relationship convert into a marriage. Hence the native under such bad influences may have to witness the loss of a beautiful and meaningful relationship which continues for many years, merely due to the interference of such malefic planets in his horoscope. In this example, if malefic Rahu is placed in the fifth house of this horoscope in the sign of Pisces when malefic retrograde Jupiter is placed in twelfth house in the sign of Libra, the lover of such native may leave him for someone else, after many years of relationship whereas if malefic Mars is present in the fifth house of the same horoscope instead of malefic Rahu, such relationship may break on account of serious misunderstandings between the native and his lover.

It means that over many years of this relationship, the couple may first develop attraction and chemistry but with the passage of time and due to these malefic influences, they may start disagreeing with each other on more and more issues and finally a day may come, when they may decide to move away from each other, unless some grace saving influence is present in the horoscope of this native. For instance, the presence of benefic Venus or benefic Moon in the fifth house of this horoscope in the sign of Pisces along with malefic Mars or malefic Rahu can still get the native married to his lover. The native under the effect of these malefic as well as benefic influences may witness serious disagreements with his lover at a time, but such differences may finally be settled and they may both get married.

Considering another example, the presence of malefic retrograde Jupiter in the twelfth house of a horoscope in the sign of Virgo may not delay the marriage of the native but it may cause different types of problems in his marriage. The native under the effect of such malefic influence may not be able to develop much bonding with his wife and he may start feeling more and more alone in her company, with the passage of time, after their marriage. This situation can become even worse if there are some other malefic influences present in his horoscope, like the presence of malefic Rahu or malefic Mercury in the seventh house of the same horoscope in the sign of Aries. In this case, the native under the combined influence of these malefic planets may get involved in an extramarital affair which may cause much trouble in his marriage and which may even break his marriage, if no strong marriage saving influence is present in his horoscope. For instance, the presence of a combination of benefic Moon and benefic Mars in the first house of this horoscope in the sign of Libra can still save the marriage of this native despite the bad influence of such malefic retrograde Jupiter and other planets.

Apart from this, malefic retrograde Jupiter placed in the twelfth house of a horoscope can cause problems in the professional sphere of the native under its influence as well as the issues related to his overall health and well being. Accordingly, some natives under this malefic influence may have to suffer on front of their professions whereas some other natives may have to face health issues or diseases due to such malefic influence. For example, the presence of malefic retrograde Jupiter in the twelfth house of a horoscope in the sign of Gemini can trouble the native with problems related to his health and accordingly the native may suffer from such issues. If malefic Rahu or malefic Moon is placed in the sixth house of this horoscope in the sign of Sagittarius, such problems may intensify and the native under the combined effect of these malefic influences may get afflicted with one or more than one permanent type of disease.

The presence of malefic Saturn in the third house of this horoscope can add more negativity to this equation and accordingly, the native under the combined effect of such malefic retrograde Jupiter and other malefic planets quoted in this example may get afflicted with some life threatening disease and he may die at a relatively young age, by virtue of this disease, if there is no other life promoting influence in the horoscope of the native. For instance, the presence of a combination of benefic Sun and benefic Mars in the first house of this horoscope or the presence of a combination of benefic Moon and benefic Mars in the first house of this horoscope can still make sure that the native lives up to a proper age, despite the malefic effect of these planets.

Retrograde Venus in 1st House

When showing retrograde in a horoscope, Venus can cause various types of positive or negative results for the native depending on its working nature, strength, level of activity and some other factors. The natives having retrograde Venus in their horoscopes may experience some of the below mentioned results depending on the placement of retrograde Venus in various houses of their horoscopes. The scope of a planet to cause various effects in any house of a horoscope is vast and it can't be contained in some words but I'll still mention some commonly occurring positive and negative effects of Venus when retrograde and placed in various houses of a horoscope.

Retrograde Venus in 1st House: When working positively, retrograde Venus placed in the first house of a horoscope can bless the native with a wide variety of benefits, comforts and pleasures related to the spheres of his marriage, profession, health, finances and many other spheres of his life. Accordingly different natives benefitting from this positive influence may experience good results related to different spheres of their lives which may vary in type and quantum, depending on the type and strength of this influence as well as depending on the overall tone of the horoscopes of these natives. Benefic retrograde Venus in the first house of a horoscope is a very good placement of this planet as far as good results in professional sphere are concerned, which means that such placement can bless the native with professional success.

Some natives benefitting from this good influence may excel and achieve success in various types of creative fields and accordingly they may become successful as movie actors, TV or stage actors, directors or some other type of people working in these fields, writers creating beautiful writings about various topics, professionals designing Video games and other high end graphic games, politicians, political leaders or diplomats who rise to high levels of fame and authority, people achieving success through various types of sports and games and many other types of professionals. Once again, the overall success achieved by any of these natives depends on the overall theme and strength of the horoscope of the native in question. This placement is also very good when it comes to render easy money, fame, pleasures and enjoyment to the native and accordingly these natives are likely to lead a life full of success and resources.

Benefic retrograde Venus in the first house of a horoscope can bless the native with various types of creative abilities and accordingly some natives under this benefic influence may engage in one of these creative fields on professional basis. For example, the presence of benefic retrograde Venus in the first house of a horoscope in the sign of Gemini can bless the native with creative abilities related to the field of acting and accordingly the native under this benefic influence may become interested in acting on various levels. However this benefic influence alone may not be sufficient to make the native a professional as well as a successful actor and it may need support from some other positive influences in the horoscope of the native. For instance, the presence of benefic Moon in the fifth house of this horoscope in the sign of Libra can improve this equation and accordingly the native under the combined effect of such benefic retrograde Venus and Moon may witness better results related to this profession.

Such native may have a very good interest in the field of acting right from the start and he may decide to engage in this field on professional basis, and so he may start working in some movies or television programs through which he may achieve some success also. If benefic Mercury is present in the eleventh house of this horoscope in the sign of Aries, this equation may improve further and the native under the combined effect of these benefic planets may achieve even more success and fame through his profession of acting. This native may especially become famous as an actor whose voice is the most prominent feature of his acting as well as that of his personality, as the combined effect of these benefic influences is likely to bless the native with a special and different type of voice which is energetic and sensitive at the same time. Accordingly this native may receive special complements related to his voice, dialogue delivery and other such aspects related to his speech.

The presence of benefic Rahu in the tenth house of this horoscope in the sign of Pisces can add even more positivity to this equation and accordingly the native under the combined effect of such benefic retrograde Venus and other benefic planets may achieve more from this profession. Such native may not only earn good amount of money and success as a lead actor in movies or in television programs, he may also receive fame and recognition for some of his works of acting. As more and more positive planets add to this equation, the amount of success and other good results experienced may also increase as the presence of more and more benefic planets in the horoscope of this native will provide more strength to such benefic retrograde Venus in the first house of his horoscope in the sign of Gemini, and accordingly it may bless the native even more.

Some natives under this benefic influence may also achieve success through politics and accordingly they may engage in politics on different levels, depending on the type and strength of this benefic placement, as well as depending on their overall horoscopes. For example, the presence of benefic retrograde Venus in the first house of a horoscope in the sign of Leo can make the native interested in politics and accordingly the native under such benefic influence may take much interest in politics though he may not directly engage in politics as this placement alone may not be sufficient to make the native an active politician. However, if benefic Sun is also present in the first house of the same horoscope in the sign of Leo along with benefic retrograde Venus, the equation can change and the native under the combined effect of these two benefic planets may actively start participating in politics on level or the other, depending on his overall horoscope.

The addition of benefic retrograde Mercury to the second house of the same horoscope in the sign of Virgo can make this equation even more productive and accordingly the native under the combined effect of all these benefic planets may witness even better results through politics. Such native may get a post of good authority in the district or even in the state body of a good political party which is well established on national basis. If benefic Rahu is present in the second, fourth, fifth, sixth, seventh, tenth or eleventh house of this horoscope, the native under the combined effect of such benefic retrograde Venus, Sun, Mercury and Rahu may witness even more success through politics and he may receive different types of benefits depending on the placement of Rahu in his horoscope, when all other benefic planets remain present in the already mentioned houses of his horoscope.

For example, the presence of benefic Rahu in the fifth house of this horoscope in the sign of Sagittarius can bless him with a post of power and authority, not only in a political party but in some government organization also, though such native is not likely to contest in a public election on state level or on some other level. It means that the combined effect of such benefic retrograde Venus and Sun in the first house, Mercury in the second house and Rahu in the fifth house of this horoscope can bless the native with a post of power and authority which is not received by virtue of winning an election but which is obtained directly, like a member or even the chairperson of some trust or board run by government, which gives the native power and authority.

For example, the native under the combined influence of these benefic planets may get appointed as a chairman of a board or trust which looks after the well being of a specific region or category of some town or city, like an improvement trust or some other trust of this type. Such trust may have a good authority over a region and it may also have a very good financial budget due to which, the native may be in a position of much authority to make plans on big levels and then implement them. However, the placement of benefic Rahu in the fourth house of the same horoscope in the sign of Scorpio can change his equation and accordingly the native under the combined effect of such benefic retrograde Venus and other benefic planets in his horoscope may achieve success through a different path. Such native may get a ticket to run for a public election on state level, on behalf of a well established political party and if the overall horoscope as well as the time is favorable, he may even win this election and he may represent a region of his state, in the state assembly.

If benefic Mars is placed in the ninth house of the same horoscope in the sign of Aries, the native may not only win a public election on state level, but he may also win an election on national level and he may represent his region in the parliament of his country. The native under the combined influence of such benefic retrograde Venus and all other benefic planets mentioned in this example may also become a minister with a state government or even with a national government, more than once in his life. If the number of positive planets in the horoscope of this native increases further, the amount of success achieved by the native may also increase accordingly.

Looking at one more variation in the same example, if benefic Rahu is placed in the sixth house of this horoscope in the sign if Capricorn when benefic retrograde Venus is placed in the first house along with benefic Sun in the sign of Leo and benefic Mercury is placed in the second house in the sign of Virgo, the native may achieve political success in yet another way. Such native under the combined effect of all these benefic influences may choose to work on the structural level of a political party and he may not be much interested in dealing with a direct post of power and authority with the government, either by virtue of winning an election or by virtue of being appointed at one such post.

However, due to the combined effect of all these benefic influences, the native may keep getting stronger and stronger within the party and he may become the state president of a well established political party or he may go even further and secure a post of high authority in the national body of a well established political party, provided his overall horoscope allows it. Apart from this, benefic retrograde Venus in first house of a horoscope can bless the native with success through many other professional spheres and accordingly different natives under this influence may achieve success through many other professional spheres, depending on the type and strength of this benefic placement as well as depending on the overall tone of their horoscopes.

Positive retrograde Venus placed in the first house of a horoscope is especially very good for marriage and married life of the native and accordingly the natives blessed by it are likely to enjoy a timely marriage and a good married life filled with many pleasures and joys, provided the overall theme of the horoscope supports a timely and good marriage. This is in fact one of the best placements of positive retrograde Venus when it comes to get good results from marriage and married life and I have observed that many natives blessed by this placement enjoy very good marriages and they get very good support and love from their spouses. For example, the presence of benefic retrograde Venus in the first house of a horoscope in the sign of Gemini can bless the native with a good and supporting life partner and accordingly the native may enjoy a good marriage.

This placement in the horoscope of a male can bless her with a wife who if very friendly, who discuss all day to day issues with native and who ensures that a positive communication channel is always open between her and her husband so that the health of the marriage may not be adversely affected by the introduction of various types of negativities, due to lack of communication between the two of them. The wife of such native plays a very important role in her life and accordingly the native may witness much better results in almost all spheres of his life, after his marriage. On the other hand, the placement of benefic retrograde Venus in the first house of the horoscope of a female native in the sign of Gemini can bless her with a well established husband who may be rich or very rich depending on the other factors and who at the same time, may give very good importance to her. It means that such female may enjoy many pleasures through such marriage and she may also get very good support from her husband provided the overall horoscope is supportive.

On the other hand, negative retrograde Venus placed in the first house of a horoscope can bring bad or very bad results to the native and accordingly some natives suffering from this placement are likely to feel the heat of this placement in various spheres of their lives. These bad results may belong to different fields of their lives like marriage, profession and other fields, and these result may also be different in type and quantum in case of different natives, depending on the type and strength of this malefic influence, as well as depending on the overall tone of the horoscopes of these natives.

This malefic placement is especially very bad for marriage and married life due to which some natives suffering from such negative retrograde Venus may have to go through one or more than one broken marriages whereas some other natives may not be able to get married till late or very late in their lives. In some extreme cases when the overall horoscope is also negative, this placement can force the native to live without a spouse, which may happen after two or three broken marriages or which may happen due to the fact that such natives may not get married, throughout their lives.

For example, the presence of malefic retrograde Venus in the first house of a horoscope in the sign of Capricorn may not only delay the marriage of the native under its influence, but it may also cause problems in the married life of the native. Accordingly, some natives under this malefic influence may have to wait till late or very late in order to get married and some of these natives may even have to suffer from broken love relationships which continue for a long time but which don't convert into marriages, due to one reason or the other. For instance, if malefic Rahu, malefic Ketu or malefic Saturn is placed in the fifth house of the same horoscope in the sign of Taurus, the native under the combined effect of such malefic retrograde Venus in the first house and one other malefic planet in the fifth house of his horoscope may have to suffer the loss of a relationship which does not convert into marriage.

Such native may engage in a long lasting and meaningful love relationship with a beautiful female, but such love relation may not convert into a marriage, due to one reason or the other, depending on the planet present in the fifth house as well as depending on the overall tone of his horoscope. However, such worst can be avoided if some other benefic planets are present in the horoscope of this native, like the presence of benefic Moon in the seventh house of this horoscope in the sign of Cancer can still get the native married, despite the effect of all these malefic planets including malefic retrograde Venus in the first house of his horoscope.

Negative retrograde Venus in first house of a horoscope can also trouble the native with problems, delays and failures in his profession and accordingly, various natives suffering from this placement may face many types of problems in their professions depending on the type and strength of this malefic influence, as well as depending on the overall tone of the horoscopes of these natives. Some natives under this bad influence may have to change their jobs time and again, due to unfavorable circumstances whereas some other natives may have to remain jobless every now and then or for a continuous long period of time. Some other natives may have to face losses, debts and even bad reputation through their professions and in some cases, such losses and bad reputation may be strong enough to put a long break to the professional life of the native in question.

Malefic retrograde Venus in first house of a horoscope is also bad for health aspect of the native under its influence and it can trouble the native through various health issues and diseases. In some extreme cases, it can reduce the lifespan of the native by inflicting him with a fatal disease which may claim his life relatively early or very early. For example, the presence of malefic retrograde Venus in the first house of a horoscope in the sign of Libra can trouble the native on account of health related problems and accordingly the native under this bad influence may suffer from health issues. If malefic Moon is present in the sixth or eight house of this horoscope, the problems of this native may increase and accordingly, he may get afflicted by some serious disease. The presence of malefic Jupiter in the third house of the same horoscope can further complicate this equation due to which the native under the combined influence of all these malefic planets may get afflicted by some life threatening disease which may claim his life at a relatively young or very young age, depending on the overall tone of his horoscope.

Retrograde Venus in 2nd House

When working positively, retrograde Venus placed in the second house of a horoscope can bless the native under its influence with good results related to many spheres of his life including his marriage, profession, overall well being, finances and other good things. Accordingly many natives under this benefic influence may witness good results related to different spheres of their lives where such good results can be different in type as well as in quantum for different natives, depending on the type and strength of this placement as well as depending on the overall tone of the horoscopes of these natives. Such benefic influence is especially very good for the professional as well as financial aspect of the native under its influence and accordingly some natives under this benefic influence may see good results related to these spheres.

For example, the presence of benefic retrograde Venus in the second house of a horoscope in the sign of Libra can bless the native with good amount of professional success and accordingly the native under this benefic influence may earn money and success through many possible professional fields, depending on the overall tone of his horoscope. Such benefic retrograde Venus in second house of a horoscope in the sign of Libra can bless the native with success through some financial field, some educational field, real estate field, hotel business, marketing and selling of various products and many other fields depending on his overall horoscope. Accordingly the native under such influence may have special talents related to one of these spheres and so he may engage in one of these fields.

If benefic Mercury is placed in the fourth house of this horoscope in the sign of Sagittarius, the native under the combined effect of these two benefic planets may engage in some type of job, practice or business related to education and he may achieve good amount of success through it. Such native may work as a teacher in some educational institution, in some college or in some university and he may earn good amount of money and recognition through such job. If benefic Moon or benefic Rahu is also placed in the fourth house of the same horoscope in the sign of Sagittarius, this equation may improve further and accordingly the good results experienced by the native under the combined effect of these three planets may increase in quantum. Such native may either become the head of staff related to a specific subject in some college or university or he may start his own educational institute which may provide tuitions as well as coaching on various subjects.

The presence of benefic Jupiter or benefic Rahu in the eleventh house of this horoscope in the sign of Cancer can add even more positivity to this equation and accordingly the native under the combined effect of such benefic retrograde Venus and other benefic planets placed in the already mentioned houses of his horoscope may witness even better results. The native benefitting from these positive influences may become the owner of an educational institute which may keep growing year after year and which may have many branches in many cities of a state or in many cities of a country, depending on his overall horoscope. Such native may earn very good amount of profits and recognition through such chain of educational institutes and he may witness very good growth with the passage of time.

However, the presence of benefic Jupiter or benefic Rahu in the tenth house of this horoscope in the sing of Gemini, instead of one of them being placed in the eleventh house of this horoscope can change these results, though all other planets including retrograde Venus may remain in the same houses as already mentioned. The native under the combined influence of this new combination of benefic planets may become the principal of a well established and famous college or he may hold a position of high authority in some well established educational institute, but he may not own such institute. It means that though this new combination can render similar or even more level of authority to the native compared to the previous combination of benefic planets, it may not bless him with the same amount of financial incomes.

If benefic Saturn is also placed in the tenth house of this horoscope in the sign of Gemini along with one more benefic planet say benefic Jupiter, the native under the combined effect of such benefic retrograde Venus and all other planets mentioned in this example may experience even better results. Such native may get appointed as a vice-chancellor of a big university or he may even hold a position of high power and authority in some educational board or advisory committee belonging to a state government or even in a committee belonging to the national government. Such native may also earn a very good reputation and he may even get some formal award for his work related to such sphere of education, provided his overall horoscope supports it.

Benefic retrograde Venus in the second house of a horoscope can also bless the native under its influence with success through the sphere of real estate and accordingly some natives under this benefic influence may engage in this field and achieve success on different levels, depending on their overall horoscopes. For example, the presence of benefic retrograde Venus in the second house of a horoscope in the sign of Libra, just like in the previous example, can also bless the native with success through the field of real estate, if the overall tone of his horoscope changes according to it. If benefic retrograde Venus is placed in the second house of a horoscope in the sign of Libra and benefic Jupiter is also placed in the second house of the same horoscope, the native under the combined effect of these benefic influences may engage in real estate business and he may earn good amount of money through it. Such native may not only witness good financial gains through this business but he may also be able to accumulate properties and wealth through this business.

The presence of benefic Sun in the eleventh house of this horoscope can change this equation slightly and accordingly the native may experience somewhat different results. The native under the combined effect of such benefic retrograde Venus, benefic Jupiter and benefic Sun may get a well settled family business dealing with real estate and he may not even have to work hard to establish it. It means that such native may join the already well established real estate business started and established by his father and he may not have to struggle at all, in order to establish it. If benefic Mercury is also placed in the eleventh house of the same horoscope along with benefic Sun in the sign of Cancer, the equation may become even more positive and the native may gain even more success.

Such native under the combined influence of all these planets may not only get a well establish real estate business through his father, but he may himself add much value to it, which means that the native may take this business to new heights and he may witness very good amount of financial gains, growth and expansion through this business. As more and more positive planets keep adding to this equation, the horoscope of this native may become more and more favorable and accordingly the native may earn more and more success through this business. For example, the presence of benefic Saturn in the sixth house of this horoscope in the sign of Aquarius can further increase the amount of success and money earned by the native and accordingly the native under the combined effect of such benefic retrograde Venus and other benefic planets may earn even more profits and success through this business.

Benefic retrograde Venus in the second house of a horoscope can also bless the native with good, very good or great amount of money through inheritance and accordingly some natives under this benefic influence may get this type of benefit also. Here again the type of inheritance as well as the quantum of inheritance gained by different natives under this benefic influence may differ depending on the type and strength of this benefic influence, as well as depending on the overall tone of the horoscopes of these natives. For example, the presence of benefic retrograde Venus in the second house of a horoscope in the sign of Gemini can bless the native with good amount of money and wealth that he may receive through his paternal family, provided his overall horoscope allows it. If benefic Moon is also present in the second house of the same horoscope in the sign of Gemini, the native under the combined effect of these benefic influences may receive very good amount of inheritance from his father's side, from his mother's side or from both the sides.

However, if in the horoscope of female, benefic retrograde Venus is placed in the second house of her horoscope in the sign of Gemini and benefic Mars is also present with it, the results may change altogether and the gains witnessed by such female may vary accordingly. Such female native under the combined effect of these benefic influences may receive a good amount of wealth through her husband which may be due to the fact that her husband dies and leaves a very good amount of money and wealth for her. Such female native may also get such money and wealth by means of a divorce settlement between her and her husband, where she gets a considerable amount of money and wealth. The chances of this happening can increase even further if benefic Rahu is also present in the second house of the same horoscope, as the combined effect of such benefic retrograde Venus, benefic Mars and benefic Rahu can bless such female native with very good amount of money and wealth through some divorce settlement, provided her overall horoscope allows it.

Benefic retrograde Venus in the second house can also bless the native under its influence with good, very good or great results related to his marriage and accordingly some natives benefitting from this positive influence may witness good results related to their marriages which may be different in type and quantum depending on the type and strength of this benefic placement, as well as depending on the overall tone of the horoscopes of these natives. Some natives under this benefic influence may get supportive and caring partners, some of them may get rich and well established partners, some of them may get married to someone settled in a foreign country and they may themselves settle in that foreign country after marriage, and some of them may get married to people who hold a position of power and authority, by virtue of this benefic placement of retrograde Venus in the second house of their horoscopes.

For example, the presence of benefic retrograde Venus in the second house of a horoscope in the sign of Taurus may get the native married to someone rich and well established from his own country or this benefic placement may bless the native with a well established life partner from a foreign country, depending on the other factors in the horoscope of this native. For instance, if in the horoscope of a male, benefic retrograde Venus is placed in the second house in the sign of Taurus, such male native may get married to a female who belongs to a rich and well established family and he may benefit from this marriage.

If benefic Jupiter is placed in the first, seventh, eighth or twelfth house of the same horoscope, the native under the combined effect of these benefic planets may get married to a girl who belongs to a foreign country and he may also get settled in that foreign country, on the basis of such marriage. Such native is likely to get good support from his wife, which means that the wife of such native may help her a lot in his professional sphere as well as in the other spheres of his life and he may witness good rise in his professional success as well as in his overall standard of living. If more benefic planets add to this equation or if some planets indicate somewhat different benefic results for this native, the native may get those results accordingly.

The same placement of benefic retrograde Venus in the second house of the horoscope of a female native can indicate somewhat different results and accordingly she may have different experience through her marriage. The presence of benefic retrograde Venus in the second house of the horoscope of female in the sign of Taurus can get her married to a rich person though this placement on its own may not guarantee a good married life and it may need support from some other good influences. If benefic Jupiter is placed in the first house of her horoscope in the sign of Aries, the female under the combined effect of these two benefic planets may not only enjoy a good marriage, but she may also experience very good changes by virtue of her marriage. It means that the overall living standard as well as the overall lifestyle of this female native may change a lot, by virtue of her marriage to a well established as well as a supportive husband. The husband of such female may guide, love and support her a lot and accordingly she may witness very good things after her marriage, provided her overall horoscope allows it.

However all is not well with this placement of retrograde Venus in the second house of a horoscope and things can go bad or very bad for the native under its influence, in many spheres of his life, if such retrograde Venus turns negative in the second house of his horoscope. Accordingly many natives suffering from this malefic placement may have to face problems related to many spheres of their lives where such problems may be different in type and quantum, depending on the type and quantum of this malefic placement, as well as depending on the overall tone of their horoscopes. Such bad influence may especially be very troublesome for marriage due to which some natives suffering from this malefic influence may have to face different types of bad results related to the sphere of their marriage. Some of these natives may not get married at proper times and they may have to wait till late or very late in order to get married whereas some other such natives may have to witness many problems and troubles through their marriages.

For example, the presence of malefic retrograde Venus in the second house of a horoscope in the sign of Scorpio can cause delay in the marriage of the native under its influence and accordingly such native may have to wait till late or very late in order to get married. If malefic Rahu, malefic Ketu or malefic Saturn is also placed in the second house of the same horoscope in the sign of Scorpio, the marriage of such native may delay even longer and accordingly the native may have to wait till 35 years of his age or even longer in order to get married. Looking at some even worse possibilities, if a combination of malefic retrograde Venus and malefic Saturn is present in the second house of a horoscope in the sign of Scorpio and a combination of malefic Mars and malefic Ketu is placed in the eighth or twelfth house of the same horoscope, the native under the combined effect of such malefic influences may not be able to get married at all, throughout his life, unless there are some other good influences in his horoscope, which promote his marriage.

Taking a look at another example, the presence of malefic retrograde Venus in the second house of a horoscope in the sign of Leo may not delay the marriage of the native under its influence, but it may cause many disturbances in the marriage of such native and accordingly the native may experience many types of problems in his marriage, depending on his overall horoscope. If malefic Saturn is also placed in the second house of the same horoscope in the sign of Leo or if malefic Saturn is placed in the sixth house of the same horoscope in the sign of Sagittarius, the combined effect of these malefic planets may break one marriage of the native. Accordingly, the native may have to face a divorce after suffering through serious problems of arguments, disagreements and lack of trust between him and his wife. If at the same time, malefic Rahu or malefic Ketu is placed in the seventh house of the same horoscope in the sign of Capricorn, the native under the combined effect of all these malefic planets may have to suffer from more than one broken marriage and he may finally be able to settle in his third or even in his fourth marriage.

Malefic retrograde Venus in the second house of a horoscope can also trouble the native on account of problems related to his profession, financial equation and his overall health. Accordingly some natives under this malefic influence may suffer on account of these problems also. For example, the presence of malefic retrograde Venus in the second house of a horoscope in the sign of Capricorn can trouble the native under its influence with problems related to his professional sphere, as well as with the problems related to his overall financial equation. Accordingly the native under such malefic influence may have to change his profession many times in his life and if there are other malefic influences in his horoscope which add more negativity to such malefic retrograde Venus, the native may also have to remain jobless for some months or even for some years, more than once in his life. For instance, the presence of malefic Saturn or malefic Ketu in the tenth house of the same horoscope can make the native remain jobless for some months or even for some years, more than once in his life.

Retrograde Venus in 3rd House

When benefic in nature, retrograde Venus placed in the third house of a horoscope can bless the native with good results related to profession, marriage, health and many other spheres of his life. These results may be different in type and quantum for different natives, depending on the type and strength of this placement as well as depending on the overall tone of the horoscopes of these natives. This benefic influence can especially be very good for the professional aspect of the native due to which many natives under the effect of this benefic influence may achieve success through a wide variety of professional spheres, depending on the overall tone of their horoscopes.

Some natives under this benefic influence may get engaged in a professional field which deals with arranging or facilitating tours and travels for other people, in one way or the other. For example, the presence of benefic retrograde Venus in the third house of a horoscope in the sign of Aquarius can make the native interested in a profession related to tours and travels like hotel booking, air ticket booking, booking and managing a complete tour and other such professional spheres. Accordingly the native may engage in one of these professional spheres if the overall tone of his horoscope is in accordance with this profession and he may achieve the amount of success allowed by his horoscope. Such native may get a job in some company dealing with tours and travels and he may earn decent amount of money through such job.

If benefic Jupiter is placed in the eleventh house of this horoscope in the sign of Libra, this equation can improve and accordingly the amount of success achieved by this native may improve. Accordingly the native under the combined effect of such benefic retrograde Venus and benefic Jupiter in the already mentioned houses of his horoscope may get a better job in the same field and he may be appointed as the head of some section in one such company. The presence of benefic Saturn in the third house of this horoscope can add more positivity to this equation and the native may benefit even more. The native under the combined effect of these three positive planets may start his own company which provides services related to tours and travels industry and he may earn good amount of money through it.

Such native may start slow and then see better results with passage of time, which means that he may have to work for some other companies in the same field for some years in order to gain experience, before he starts his own company. Such company may take some time to establish and accordingly the native may have to wait for some years in order to see good results, but finally his business may start fetching him more money, more success and more growth with the passage of time. If benefic Mercury is present in the ninth house of this horoscope in the sign of Leo or if benefic Rahu is placed in the first or twelfth house of this horoscope, the equation may become even better and the native may witness much better results.

The native under the combined effect of these benefic influences may witness much more success through such business and such success may now come at a fast pace, which means the native may not have to wait for some years in order to see good results from his business and he may start getting good results soon after the start of his business. If benefic retrograde Venus and benefic Saturn are placed in the third house of a horoscope in the sign of Aquarius, benefic Jupiter is placed in the eleventh house of the same horoscope in sign of Libra, benefic Mercury is placed in the ninth house of this horoscope in the sign of Leo and benefic Rahu is placed in the twelfth house of this horoscope in the sign of Scorpio, the amount of success achieved by the native may increase even more.

Accordingly, the native under the combined effect of all these benefic influences may start his business related to this field, which provides services and arrangements related to tours and travels within his country, but he may soon expand his business on international level. It means that such native may become the head of a company which deals with international tours and travels management like hotel booking, arranging Visas, air ticket booking, site seeing and all other such services which generally come in a travel package. The native under the benefic influence of all these benefic planets may earn very good amount of money and success through such business and he may keep growing more and more with the passage of time. As more and more positive planets keep adding to this equation, the native under the combined effect of all these benefic planets may achieve even more success through this line of profession.

Some natives under this benefic influence may also get interested in the professional fields which deal with improvement, enhancement or transformation of human body on different levels and accordingly these natives may become professionals like gym trainers, yoga instructors, Aerobics teachers and other professionals of the similar kind. These natives may achieve different type and amount of success depending on the type and strength of his benefic influence, as well as depending on the overall tone of their horoscopes. For example, the presence of benefic retrograde Venus in the third house of a horoscope in the sign of Libra can make the native interested in one such field and accordingly the native may engage in one such profession, let's say the native becomes a gym instructor.

If benefic Mercury or benefic Rahu is also present in the third house of the same horoscope in the sign of Libra along with such benefic retrograde Venus, the combined effect of both these benefic planets can bless the native with better results. Accordingly the native may get appointed as a gym trainer in a more established gym and he may earn more money through such job. The presence of benefic Jupiter in the eleventh house of the same horoscope may add more positivity to this equation due to which the native under the combined effect of all these benefic planets may not only become a gym instructor in a very well established gym, but he may earn very good amount of money and good amount of recognition through personal trainings. It means that apart from earning his regular salary, such native may get many personal trainees who may add much more money to the monthly income of this native. This native may also be able to project a very good image of himself as a trainer, as many of the clients trained by him may witness very good results and they may refer him to more and more people, who need such services.

Considering one more possibility in the same example, if benefic retrograde Venus is present in the third house of a horoscope in the sign of Libra along with benefic Rahu and a combination of benefic Jupiter and benefic Mercury is placed in the eleventh house of the same horoscope in the sign of Gemini, the equation may become even better and accordingly the results may become even more positive. The native under the combined effect of all these benefic planets in various houses of his horoscope may now become the owner of a gym instead of working as a gym trainer, though he may work as a trainer for some years in a gym and then he may decide to open his own gym. The combined effect of these benefic planets is also capable of blessing the native with good results through such business and if there are more positive influences in his horoscope, the native may achieve even more success through such business of gym.

For instance, the presence of benefic Mars in the ninth house of the same horoscope in the sign of Aries or the presence of benefic Sun in the tenth house of the same horoscope in the sign of Taurus can add more positivity to the equation and accordingly the results may improve. The native under the combined effect of such benefic retrograde Venus and other benefic planets in various houses of his horoscope may start a gym of his own, which may not only witness good profits, but which may also witness good growth with the passage of time. It means the native may become the owner of a chain of gyms in a specific region, as he keeps opening more and more gyms with the passage of time, under the combined effect of all these benefic influences. As more and more positive planets keep adding to the equation, the results received by the native under the combined effect of all these benefic influences may also improve more and more, provided the overall horoscope of the native allows those results.

Taking a look at another variation in the same example, if instead of being placed in the sign of Libra, benefic retrograde Venus is placed in the third house of a horoscope in the sign of Cancer and there are some other supportive factors in the horoscope, the native may become a yoga instructor or a teacher who teaches meditation techniques for self improvement, instead of become a gym trainer. For example, if benefic retrograde Venus is present in the third house of a horoscope in the sign of Cancer and at the same time, benefic Jupiter is placed in the first house of the same horoscope in the sign of Taurus, the native may become a yoga instructor and he may achieve good amount of success through such profession.

However, if benefic retrograde Venus is placed in the third house of a horoscope in the sign of Cancer and either benefic Moon is also present in the third house of the same horoscope in the sign of Cancer or benefic Mars is present in the first house of this horoscope in the sign of Taurus, the native under the combined effect of these benefic influences may become a teacher in meditation techniques for self improvement. If however, benefic retrograde Venus is placed in the third house of a horoscope in the sign of Cancer, benefic Mars is placed in the first house of the same horoscope in the sign of Taurus and benefic Moon is placed in the twelfth house of this horoscope in the sign of Aries, the native under the combined effect of these benefic influences may become a spiritual guru or spiritual teacher, instead of become a yoga instructor or a teacher who teaches meditation techniques for self improvement. Astrology is full of possibilities and accordingly even smallest of the changes in any aspect of a horoscope can change the final outcome.

Benefic retrograde Venus in the third house of a horoscope can also bless the native with good results in marriage and accordingly some natives benefitting from this positive influence may witness various types of good results through their marriages, depending on the type and strength of this benefic influence as well as depending on the overall tone of their horoscopes. Some natives under the effect of this benefic influence may get married to well established life partners who may also be supportive and helping towards these natives due to which, these natives may enjoy a better quality of professional as well as general life after marriage. For example, the presence of benefic retrograde Venus in the third house of a horoscope in the sign of Leo can bless the native with a well established and supportive life partner. The presence of such benefic influence in the horoscope of a male can bless her with a supportive and adaptive wife who may come from a rich and well established family whereas the presence of such benefic influence in the horoscope of a female native can bless her with a rich or well established husband.

The husband of such female native may love and support her to a good extent and she may also be able to witness rise in her professional as well as in her social graph, by virtue of the support and guidance provided by her husband. As more and more positive factors keep appearing in the horoscope of such male or female native, the results witnessed by them may also improve. For example, the presence of benefic Moon along with benefic retrograde Venus in the third house of a horoscope in the sign of Leo can bless the native with even better results and the presence of benefic Jupiter in the first or eleventh house of the same horoscope can further bless the native with some of the best possible results through his marriage. Such native may achieve much prosperity, growth and social status after his marriage, apart from enjoying a very good marriage, as the combined effect of all these benefic planets is fully capable of blessing the native with some of the best possible results through marriage, provided his overall horoscope supports such results.

On the other hand, retrograde Venus placed in the third house of a horoscope can trouble the native with problems in many spheres of his life, if it turns negative in a horoscope. Accordingly some natives under this malefic influence may have to face problems in their marriage, profession, health and many other aspects of their lives where the type and intensity of such problems may be different for different natives, depending on the type and strength of this malefic influence as well as depending on the overall tone of the horoscopes of these natives. Malefic retrograde Jupiter in the third house of a horoscope can trouble the native with some of the most serious types of health related problems and accordingly some natives under this bad influence may suffer from various types of health issues and diseases, depending on their overall horoscopes.

For example, the presence of malefic retrograde Venus in the third house of a horoscope in the sign of Cancer can trouble the native with health related issues which may be different in case of different natives depending on many important factors. The presence of such malefic influence in the third house of the horoscope of a male native in the sign of Cancer can trouble him with health problems and diseases related to his nervous system or with problems which are psychological in nature, among many other types of diseases. On the other hand, the presence of such malefic retrograde Venus in the third house of the horoscope of a female native in the sign of Cancer can trouble her with issues related to her reproductive system. Accordingly this female native may experience delay or change in length of her periods or she may witness excessive pain or bleeding during her periods depending on the other factors in her horoscopes.

Such female native may also have to face problems and medical complications when it comes to conceive and deliver a child and hence she may have to face delay in child birth and she may also have to undergo medical treatment in order to be able to conceive and deliver a child. If there are other malefic influences in her horoscope, the situation may become even more complicated and accordingly she may to suffer even more. For example, if malefic retrograde Venus is present in the third house of her horoscope in the sign of Cancer and malefic Saturn, Rahu, Ketu or Mars is present in the fifth house of her horoscope, the female native under the combined effect of these malefic influences may have to face even more medical complications related to her reproductive system and accordingly she may have to witness even more delay in child birth or she may also have to face some abortions.

Malefic retrograde Venus in the third house of a horoscope can also cause problems in the professional sphere of the native under its influence and accordingly some natives suffering from this bad influence may have to face different kinds of problems in their professions, depending on the type and strength of this malefic placement, as well as depending on the overall tone of the horoscopes of these natives. For example, malefic retrograde Venus placed in the third house of a horoscope in the sign of Sagittarius can not only cause delays and disturbances in the professional sphere of the native, but such malefic influence can also render criminal tendencies to the native. Accordingly, some natives under the bad effect of this malefic influence may tend to engage in crimes and they may actively engage in various crimes if there are some other negative influences in their horoscopes. For instance, if malefic Rahu is placed in the first, third, sixth, eighth, tenth or eleventh house of the same horoscope, the native under the combined effect of these malefic planets may actively engage in various types of crimes depending on the placement of malefic Rahu in his horoscope.

While the presence of malefic Rahu in the first house of this horoscope in the sign of Libra along with the presence of malefic retrograde Venus in the third house of this horoscope in the sign of Sagittarius can make the native engage in financial types of crimes, the presence of malefic Rahu in the third house of this horoscope along with malefic retrograde Venus in the sign of Sagittarius can make him engage in some crimes related to the smuggling and selling of various types of drugs or he may engage in some type of crimes which deal in direct violence. Similarly, the presence of malefic Rahu in the sixth house of this horoscope can make the native engage in white collar crimes which means such native may engage in various crimes but he may not engage in them openly, whereas the presence of such malefic Rahu in the tenth house of the same horoscope can make him a declared criminal.

It means that if malefic retrograde Venus is present in the third house of a horoscope in the sign of Sagittarius and malefic Rahu is present in the tenth house of this horoscope in the sign of Cancer, the native may not believe in being a white collar criminal and on the contrary, he may become the one who feels proud to be a criminal. Such native may tell other people about his accomplishments in the life of crime with great pride and he is not likely to be ashamed of being a criminal at all. If malefic Jupiter or malefic Moon is placed in the sixth or twelfth house of the same horoscope, the native under the combined effect of these malefic planets may have to spend many years of his life in some prison, by virtue of some crimes committed by him. As more and more negative influences keep adding to this equation, the native under the combined effect of such malefic influences including malefic retrograde Venus in the third house of his horoscope may have to suffer more and more through such life of crime.

Retrograde Venus in 4th House

When working positively in a horoscope, benefic retrograde Venus placed in fourth house of a horoscope can render a variety of good results to the native under its influence and accordingly different natives benefitting from this good influence may profit on the front of their marriage, profession, financial status, wealth, luxury and many other spheres of their lives. The type and quantum of results experienced by different natives under this benefic influence may be different depending on the type and strength of this benefic influence as well as depending on the overall tone of the horoscopes of these natives.

Some natives under the effect of this benefic influence may experience good, very good or great results related to their professional spheres depending on their overall horoscopes. For example, the presence of benefic retrograde Venus in the fourth house of a horoscope in the sign of Leo can make the native interested in some type of government services which offer power and authority and accordingly the native under the effect of such influence may think of joining one such service in some government department. However, this benefic influence alone may not be sufficient to bless the native with good results in this sphere and it may need support from other good influences in his horoscope. If benefic Saturn is placed in the tenth house of this horoscope in the sign of Aquarius, the native under the combined effect of both these benefic planets may get selected in some government service which offers good power and authority and he may enjoy good amount of success and resources through this post.

The presence of benefic Moon in the first house of the same horoscope in the sign of Taurus can add more positivity to this equation due to which the native may witness even more success. The native under the combined effect of such benefic retrograde Venus, benefic Saturn and benefic exalted Moon in the already mentioned houses of his horoscope may directly get selected for a very high post of power and authority in some government department and he may also enjoy a good career filled with promotions, achievements, recognition and many other types of benefits, provided his overall horoscope allows it. If benefic Sun is present in the ninth house of the same horoscope in the sign of Capricorn, the combined effect of all these benefic planets can render even more success to the native.

Accordingly the native benefitting from all these positive planets may get selected for some government job at the highest possible direct rank in a government department and he may also enjoy a very good career. The addition of benefic retrograde Mercury to the tenth house of this horoscope in the sign of Capricorn can make this equation even better and accordingly the native under the combined effect of such benefic retrograde Venus, Saturn, Moon, Sun and Mercury in the already mentioned houses of this horoscope may witness even better results. Such native may have an exceptional career record and he may serve for many years at the top of his department, before he is retired.

For instance, if this native becomes a police officer by virtue of all these benefic placements, he may serve as the chief of police for an entire state for some years before he is finally retired. If such native becomes an administrative officer under the combined effect of all these benefic influences, he may get the honor of becoming the principal secretary of an entire state or that of even an entire country, if his overall horoscope allows it. The native under the combined influence of all these benefic planets may also achieve much recognition and some formal awards for his exceptional services to his department. As more and more positive planets keep adding to this equation, the native under the combined effect of all these benefic influences may achieve even more success.

Benefic retrograde Venus placed in the fourth house of a horoscope can also bless the native with success through hotel industry and accordingly some natives benefitting from this positive influence may achieve good results through this industry on different levels, depending on their overall horoscopes. For example, the presence of benefic retrograde Venus in the fourth house of a horoscope in the sign of Cancer can make the native interested in joining some job related to this industry and he may even do so, if his overall horoscope allows it. The presence of benefic Saturn or benefic Ketu in the eleventh house of the same horoscope can supply the required push and accordingly the native under the combined effect of these benefic planets may get a decent job in hotel industry. The native under the combined effect of such benefic retrograde Venus and benefic Ketu in third and eleventh house of his horoscope respectively, is likely to get a job related to hospitality or management of some type. It means that such native may become a receptionist, some other type of caretaker or even a manager in some hotel, depending on the overall tone of his horoscope.

However, if benefic retrograde Venus is placed in the fourth house of a horoscope in the sign of Cancer and benefic Saturn is placed in the second house of the same horoscope, the native under the combined influence of these benefic planets may instead become a cook or a chef and he may get a relevant job in the same line, in some hotel. The type of job title this native gets, the class of hotel that hires this native and the type of success and income he gets, it all depends on the overall tone of his horoscope. Taking a look at one more possible combination belonging to the same line, if benefic retrograde Venus is placed in the fourth house of a horoscope and benefic Saturn is also placed in the same house of this horoscope in the sign of Cancer, the native under the combined effect of these two benefic planets may start his career as a manager in some hotel and he may get promoted to better and better hotels with the passage of time. If the overall horoscope of this native is supportive, he may become the general manager of a four star or even a five star hotel, by virtue of the combined effect of these two benefic planets in his horoscope.

Introducing yet another possibility to this equation, if benefic retrograde Venus and benefic Saturn are placed in the fourth house of a horoscope in the sign of Cancer and benefic Moon is placed in the second house of the same horoscope in the sign of Taurus, the native under the combined effect of these benefic planets may start his own hotel, instead of working at other people's hotels. If benefic Jupiter or benefic Rahu is present in the eleventh house of the same horoscope in the sign of Aquarius, the native under the combined effect of all these benefic planets may witness even better results from this profession. Such native may start from one hotel which may do very good business over the years and the native may start more hotels with the passage of time, inspired by the success achieved through his first hotel.

The presence of benefic Sun in the ninth house of this horoscope can add even more to this equation and accordingly the results may improve even more. The native under the combined effect of such benefic retrograde Venus and other benefic planets may become the owner of a well reputed chain of hotels and he may earn very good amount of profits and fame through such chain of hotels. If benefic Mars is present in the twelfth house of the same horoscope in the sign of Pisces, the native under the combined effect of these benefic planets may not achieve success on national level, but he may witness success on international level also. It means that the native may own a well reputed and well established chain of hotels, which may not only mark its presence in his own country, but it may also open many branches in some foreign countries.

Benefic retrograde Venus in the fourth house of a horoscope can also render good results related to many fields associated with the domain of spiritualism, paranormal and other such domains. Accordingly, different natives benefitting from this good influence may witness different type and different quantum of results related to these spheres depending on their overall horoscopes. For example, the presence of benefic retrograde Venus in the fourth house of a horoscope in the sign of Virgo can render special abilities and interests related to the fields of spiritualism as well as paranormal, to the native under its influence. Accordingly the native under this benefic influence may get interested in one of these fields and he may conduct studies and even researches related to one such field, as allowed by the overall tone of his horoscope.

It should be noted that though Venus is debilitated in the sign of Virgo, it is still capable of blessing the native with good amount of benefits related to one of these fields, if it is working benefic in the horoscope and there are some other supportive influences in the horoscope of the native. Let's now look at some different possible combinations of benefic planets in the same horoscope and try to understand how the changes in placements and combinations of other planets in this horoscope can influence the final results received by the native. If benefic retrograde Venus is present in the fourth house of a horoscope in the sign of Virgo and benefic Mercury is also present in the same house and in the same sign, such combination of these two benefic planets is more likely to bend the native towards some faith like astrology, numerology or even some type of field related to the teaching of yoga, instead of making him interested in a direct line related to spiritualism.

Accordingly the native under the combined influence of these benefic planets may get more and more interested in one such line and he may also engage in it on professional basis, if his overall horoscope allows it. For instance, the presence of benefic Mars in the sixth house of the same horoscope in the sign of Scorpio can make the native pursue a career in the practice of astrology and accordingly the native under the combined effect of these benefic influences may become a professional astrologer. At the same time, if benefic Jupiter is present in the first, fifth, sixth, tenth or eleventh house of this horoscope, the native may earn good amount of money, success, recognition and fame as an astrologer, depending on the placement of such benefic Jupiter in his horoscope.

For example, the presence of benefic Jupiter in the fifth house of this horoscope can bless the native with more fame and money but it may not render very good amount of actual knowledge related to this field of astrology whereas the presence of benefic Jupiter in the sixth house or tenth house of this horoscope can bless the native with more success as an astrologer, but the native may earn comparatively less, compared to the placement of Jupiter in the fifth house of his horoscope. Moving on, the presence of benefic Jupiter in the eleventh house of the same horoscope in the sign of Aries can prove to be the best placement of this benefic planet in this horoscope and accordingly the native may see different results, compared to other placements of such benefic Jupiter.

The native under the combined effect of such benefic retrograde Venus and benefic Mercury in the fourth house of his horoscope in the sign of Virgo, benefic Mars in the sixth house of his horoscope in the sign of Scorpio and benefic Jupiter in the eleventh house of his horoscope in the sign of Aries may not only earn good amount of money, fame and recognition as an astrologer, but he may actually be blessed with good level of knowledge related to this field. It means that the native under the combined effect of all these benefic influences may not only be able to attract more and more clients, he may also be able to solve many of their problems by virtue of such good amount of knowledge possessed by him. The addition of more and more positive planets in different houses of the same horoscope, like the presence of benefic Sun in the third house of this horoscope or the presence of benefic Saturn in the eighth or ninth house of this horoscope can further improve the results achieved by this native.

Let's now discus one more possible set of arrangements of different planets in the same horoscope and see what may happen in this case. If benefic retrograde Venus is placed in the fourth house of a horoscope in the sign of Virgo and benefic Moon is present in the tenth house of this horoscope in the sign of Pisces, the native under the combined effect of these benefic influences may become more interested in some line directly related to the field of spiritual growth and accordingly he may conduct studies and researches in one such line. If benefic Mercury is placed in the eighth house of this horoscope in the sign of Capricorn, the native under the combined effect of these benefic planets may become a teacher who teaches different techniques of spiritual meditation and other such things which can help people achieve spiritual advancement. If benefic Saturn is placed in the eighth, ninth or tenth house of this horoscope, the native under the combined effect of all these benefic planets including benefic retrograde Venus in fourth house of his horoscope may experience even better results through the same line.

On the other hand, malefic retrograde Venus placed in the fourth house of a horoscope can trouble the native on many fronts of his life and accordingly different natives suffering from this malefic influence may have to face problems in the sphere of marriage, profession, health, finances and many other spheres of their lives. Here again, the type of bad results as well as the intensity of bad results experienced by different natives may be different depending on the type and strength of this malefic influence, as well as depending on the overall tone of the horoscopes of these natives. Some natives under this malefic influence may suffer from various health related issues and diseases which may differ in type and intensity based on the overall horoscopes of these natives. For example, the presence of malefic retrograde Venus in the fourth house of a horoscope in the sign of Capricorn can trouble the native on account of health related problems and accordingly the native under the effect of this malefic influence may have to suffer on account of his health.

The presence of malefic Jupiter, malefic Rahu or malefic Ketu in the same house of this horoscope in the sign of Capricorn can further intensify this problem and accordingly the native under the combined effect of these malefic planets may suffer from some disease which is considered serious in intensity. If a combination of malefic retrograde Venus and malefic Rahu is placed in the fourth house of a horoscope in the sign of Capricorn and malefic Jupiter is placed in the third house of the same horoscope in the sign of Sagittarius, the native under the combined effect of these malefic planets may suffer from a very serious disease.

It means that such native may suffer from some type of tumors in some part of his body or from some type of cancer which may inflict the native again and again due to which the native may have to undergo many surgeries at different times, in order to get rid of such tumors. If there are other malefic influences present in the horoscope of this native, which combine with the negative effect of these malefic influences, and there are no major life saving planets in the horoscope of this native, such native may die by virtue of such disease, after suffering a lot for a long period of time. Apart from this, malefic retrograde Venus in the fourth house of a horoscope can trouble the native with many other types of health issues and diseases, some of which may prove fatal for the native, if such malefic retrograde Venus is supported by some other malefic planets in the horoscope of the native.

Some natives under the effect of this malefic influence can also face problems related to their marriages where these problems can be of different types and different intensities for different natives, depending on the type and strength of this malefic influence, as well as depending on the overall tone of the horoscopes of these natives. For example, the presence of malefic retrograde Venus in the fourth house of a horoscope in the sign of Scorpio can delay the marriage of the native under its influence and accordingly the native under this bad influence may have to wait till late in his life, in order to get marriage. If at the same time, malefic Saturn or malefic Ketu is present in the seventh house of the same horoscope in the sign of Aquarius, the native under the combined effect of these malefic influences may be able to get married very late in his life. If there are some other malefic influences present in the horoscope of this native, he may not be able to get married at all throughout his life, unless there are some combinations present in his horoscope, which promote his marriage.

Taking another example, the presence of malefic retrograde Venus in the fourth house of a horoscope in the sign of Libra may not delay the marriage of the native under its impact but it may cause problems in the marriage of such native.

Accordingly the native suffering from such malefic influence may have to witness disturbances, heated arguments, verbal and even physical abuse through such marriage, depending on the overall tone of his horoscope. If a combination of malefic Rahu and malefic Saturn is placed in the sixth house of the same horoscope in the sign of Sagittarius, this problem may intensify even more. The native under the combined effect of all these malefic planets may have to face one or even more than one divorce after suffering a lot in his marriages, and he may only be able to settle in his second or third marriage, that too with some compromises. Apart from this, malefic retrograde Venus in fourth house of a horoscope can cause problems related to professional sphere, financial equation and many other spheres of a native's life, depending on the type and strength of this malefic influence as well as depending on the overall tone of the horoscope of such native.

Retrograde Venus in 5th House

When benefic in nature, retrograde Venus placed in the fifth house of a horoscope can bless the native with good results related to the spheres of marriage, profession, education, children, fame, prosperity, spiritualism and many other spheres of his life. Accordingly many natives under the effect of this benefic influence may witness these results where the type and quantum of these results may be different for different natives, depending on the type and strength of this benefic influence as well as depending on the overall tone of the horoscopes of these natives.

Benefic retrograde Venus in the fifth house of a horoscope can render good results related to the education aspect, to the native under its influence and hence some natives under this good influence may witness good results related to the sphere of their education, particularly their higher education. This benefic placement can render good or very good amount of intelligence and quick understanding to the native under its influence and accordingly the native may understand even the difficult looking subjects with ease. Hence the native may perform well or very well at studies and he may achieve high or very high level of formal academic education, depending on the overall tone of his horoscope. For example, the presence of benefic retrograde Venus in the fifth house of a horoscope in the sign of Gemini can bless the native with good education and such native may perform well at studies right from his early years, provided his overall horoscope allows it.

If benefic Rahu, benefic Jupiter or benefic Mars is also present in the fifth house of this horoscope in the sign of Gemini, the combined effect of these two benefic planets can bless the native with even better results in the sphere of his education and such native may achieve a degree of very high level in formal education. If a combination of benefic Venus, benefic Jupiter and benefic Rahu is present in the fifth house of a horoscope in the sign of Gemini, the native under the combined effect of these three benefic planets may even achieve the highest degree of formal education, in some subject. Such native is likely to perform exceptionally well at his studies and his performance may become even better if benefic Sun is present in the fourth house of the same horoscope in the sign of Taurus. However if instead of benefic Sun, benefic Saturn is present in the fourth house of this horoscope in the sign of Taurus, the native may go abroad in order to pursue his higher studies and if there are other supportive combinations in his horoscope, he may even settle abroad on professional basis, by virtue of such higher study.

Benefic retrograde Venus in the fifth house of a horoscope can also bless the native with good results related to love life and in fact this is one of the best placements of this planet when it comes to bless a native with a good love life. Accordingly some natives benefitting from this good influence may witness good, very good or great results related to their love lives depending on the type and strength of this benefic placement, as well as depending on the overall tone of the horoscopes of these natives. For example, the presence of benefic retrograde Venus in the fifth house of a horoscope in the sign of Capricorn can bless the native with a caring, strong and supportive type of lover who may finally get married to this native, after continuing this love affair for a reasonably long period of time. The native under the good effect of such benefic influence may get much pleasure and many benefits through such love affair as well as through such marriage, provided his overall horoscope allows it.

Looking at one more variation of this placement, the presence of benefic retrograde Venus in the fifth house of a horoscope in the sign of Pisces can bless the native with a number of benefits through his lover and such benefic influence can especially give very good results in case of female natives. A female native under the effect of this benefic influence may engage in a love relationship with a male who may either be rich and well established or who may belong to a foreign country or both of these conditions may come true. It means that such female native may even engage in a love affair with a well established man from a foreign country and she may experience much pleasure, love and growth through such relationship.

But this is not all that this benefic influence may offer and the female native under the effect of such benefic retrograde Venus in the fifth house of her horoscope in the sign of Pisces may get married to her lover after enjoying her love relationship for a long period of time and she may witness very good rise in her standard of living by virtue of such marriage. Such female native may also give birth to beautiful children with certain special abilities like creative abilities or administrative abilities and she may also witness profits and pleasures through her children, provided her overall horoscope allows all this. The presence of benefic Moon or benefic Jupiter in the fifth house of the same horoscope can enhance her fortune many times and accordingly she may witness even better results through her marriage.

However if benefic retrograde Venus is placed in the fifth house of a horoscope and benefic Mercury is also placed in the same house of this horoscope in the sign of Pisces, the native under the combined effect of these planets may witness different types of results. Such combination in the horoscope of a male native can make her engage in a relationship with a rich and divorced female or it can make the native engage in a relationship with a rich but married female. If the overall horoscope of the native allows, he may get married to this female and enjoy his fair share of her money which may be big or very big depending on the other aspects of his horoscope. If there are no planetary combinations in the horoscope of this native which support such marriage, this relationship may come to an end after continuing for many years. But even in this case, the native may witness surprising amount of financial gains through such female who may keep showering her with gifts and financial support, throughout the relationship and even after that, depending on the overall tone of the horoscope of such native.

Benefic retrograde Venus in the fifth house of a horoscope can also bless the native under its influence with good, very good or great results related to his children aspect and accordingly some natives under this benefic influence may witness good results in this field also. Once again, such good results may be different for different natives depending on the type and strength of this benefic influence as well as depending on the overall tone of horoscopes of these natives. For example, the presence of benefic retrograde Venus in the fifth house of a horoscope in the sign of Capricorn can bless the native with children who may possess very good administrative and management skills whereas the presence of benefic retrograde Venus in the fifth house of a horoscope in the sign of Leo can bless the native with children who may have special creative abilities or political wisdom and accordingly such children may excel in these fields.

The presence of benefic retrograde Venus in the fifth house of a horoscope can prove to be an excellent position of this planet when it comes to the professional success of the native under its influence and accordingly some many natives blessed by this good influence may witness good results through many different professional spheres. The type of good results and the quantum of those results may be different for different natives under this influence depending on the type and strength of this benefic placement as well as depending on the overall tone of the horoscopes of these natives. Some natives under this benefic influence may pursue a career in the field of personality development, self-improvement, motivational speaking, personal transformation coaching and other similar fields and they may achieve good, very good or great amount of professional success through one such profession.

For example, the presence of benefic retrograde Venus in the fifth house of a horoscope in the sign of Pisces can render specific type of intelligence, the ability to understand human psychology and other such abilities to the native, which can help him engage in a professional sphere which deals with improving the personalities of other people in one way or the other. Accordingly the native under this benefic influence may get interested in these topics more and more, though this benefic placement alone may not be sufficient to make the native engage in one of these fields on professional basis, and it may need more support from the horoscope of such native. If a combination of benefic Sun and benefic Mercury is present in the sixth house of this horoscope in the sign of Aries, the native under the combined influence of all these benefic planets may just get sufficient amount of positive energy to engage in one such field on professional basis and accordingly he may become one such professional, let's say a personality developer.

This native may earn good amount of success and fame through this profession and if benefic Rahu is placed in the tenth house of this horoscope in the sign of Leo, this equation may improve further. Accordingly the native under the combined effect of such benefic retrograde Venus, Sun,

Mercury and Rahu may witness more fame and recognition as a personality developer. At the same time, if benefic Saturn is placed in the ninth house of this horoscope in the sign of Cancer, the native under the combined effect of these benefic influences may also write one or more than one book on this topic and he may earn very good amount of profits and fame through such books. The presence of benefic Moon in the eighth, ninth or tenth house of this horoscope can further improve this situation and the placement of benefic Jupiter in first, fifth, ninth, tenth, eleventh or twelfth house of this horoscope can make the results even better. Accordingly, the native blessed by all these benefic planets including benefic retrograde Venus in the fifth house of his horoscope may achieve success and fame on international level and he may even become an iconic figure of his professional field.

However all is not well with this placement of retrograde Venus in the fifth house of a horoscope and it can trouble the native on almost every front of his life, if such retrograde Venus goes malefic in the fifth house of a horoscope. Accordingly many natives suffering from this malefic influence may feel the heat of this placement in different spheres of their lives including marriage, love life, profession, finances, children, education and many other spheres. Once again, different natives under the effect of this malefic influence may witness bad results which may be different in type and intensity depending on the type and strength of such malefic placement as well as depending on the overall tone of the horoscopes of these natives. Some natives suffering from this bad influence may have to face setbacks and failures in their love life, where such setbacks and failures may be different for different natives depending on their overall horoscopes.

For example, the presence of malefic retrograde Venus in the fifth house of a horoscope in the sign of Sagittarius can make the native suffer from a setback and heartbreak on the hands of his lover and accordingly the native under such malefic influence may have to witness this type of trouble in his life. Such native may engage in a love relationship with someone and the relation may continue for many years. Though the relationship may start good or very good, it may start getting sour with the passage of time and particularly from the time when the native asks his lover to marry him after some years of a solid relationship. The lover of such native may start finding excuses to postpone the decision on marriage, due to which some arguments may start over the decision of marriage as well as over the whole existence of their relationship and finally, the lover may simply refuse to get married on account of one reason or other.

The native may feel cheated and he may not be able to recover from this shock for many years of his life as this relationship meant a lot to him and he didn't expect such behavior from his lover's side. The influence of such malefic retrograde Venus in the fifth house of a horoscope in the sign of Sagittarius can make the native engage in a love relationship with a person who doesn't want to take it to the end and who is in it just for some temporary benefits. The other person is well aware of this fact right from the start and accordingly he or she doesn't commit or attach that much to the relationship whereas the native may entirely commit himself to this relationship and the denial for marriage at a later stage may come as a shock to him, which may upset him a lot. This example mentions the native as a male native due to some grammatical limitations but the same can happen to female natives also, who are under the effect of such malefic influence in the fifth house of their horoscopes.

Taking a look at another possible setback that can be caused by virtue of this malefic influence, the presence of malefic retrograde Venus in the fifth house of a horoscope in the sign of Taurus can trouble the native under its influence in a different way. The native under the effect of such malefic influence may engage in a love relationship with a female who may be very beautiful and who may look too good for this native right from the start. The native may find himself lucky to have such lover in his life and this relationship may continue for a period of time which may be for some months or even for a couple of years. However, with the passage of time, this girl may start troubling the native with increasing number of demands for materialistic things which may be too difficult for this native to manage or arrange.

Hence tensions may start rising between the two of them as the girl may be much more ambitious on materialistic front, than the native may have configured at the beginning of this relationship. Finally a day comes, when the native may either learn from someone or the girl may herself come to him and tell him that she is in a relationship with another man for some time, and she wants to put an end to her relationship with the native. The girl leaves the native for this new guy and the native feels cheated on the hands of his girlfriend. Though the girlfriend may get settled in her life in a way that she wants, the native may take many years of his life to come out of this deception.

Malefic retrograde Venus in the fifth house of a horoscope can also cause problems related to the sphere of children and accordingly some natives suffering from this bad influence may have to face many types of problems related to this sphere also. Such malefic influence can especially prove troublesome when it happens to be in the horoscope of a female due to which, the female natives under such malefic influence are likely to suffer more, compared to male natives under the same malefic influence. For example, the presence of malefic retrograde Venus in the fifth house of a horoscope in the sign of Aquarius can trouble the native with issues related to her reproductive organs or working of such reproductive organs. Accordingly such female native may experience problems related to her monthly periods where such problems can be excessive bleeding, excessive pain, delay in periods, irregular periods and other similar problems.

Hence the female native suffering from some of these issues may not be able to conceive a child in a normal way and she may have to undergo medical treatment in order to get her problems fixed and then conceive a child. At the same time, if malefic Sun or malefic Ketu is also placed in the fifth house of this horoscope in the sign of Aquarius along with malefic retrograde Venus, the problems of this female native may increase many times and accordingly she may have to suffer much more. The female native in this case may have to undergo prolonged medical treatments in order to conceive a child and she may also have to face complications during her period of pregnancy, which may also lead to the abortion of her child, more than once in her life. It means that though she may still deliver children after medical treatment, the number of her aborted children may be more than the number of her living children.

This situation can become even more complicated if a combination of malefic retrograde Venus and malefic Sun is present in the fifth house of a horoscope in the sign of Aquarius and at the same time, a combination of malefic Ketu and Moon is present in the second house or twelfth house of this horoscope. The female native under the combined influence of these malefic planets may not be able to have any child at all, despite all the medical treatments and she may have to remain childless throughout her life, unless there are some other child promoting combinations in her horoscope. Such female native may not only have to suffer a lot by not having a child despite her best efforts, she may also have to face many health issues and serious diseases which can trouble her a lot. Many of these diseases may have their center around her reproductive region and accordingly she may have to get her uterus removed after serious and recurring infections in it or she may have to face other medical problems related to or around her reproductive system.

Malefic retrograde Venus in the fifth house of a horoscope can also trouble the native on the front of his education, health, profession, reputation and many other things. Accordingly some natives under this malefic influence may have to face problems in some of these fields also, depending on their overall horoscopes. Some natives under this malefic influence may have to face problems in their professional sphere like some of them may not be able to find suitable jobs or professions till late or very late in their lives. Some other such natives may not find well paying job according to their qualifications or talents and they may have to adjust with low paying and low standard jobs by virtue of this malefic influence. Yet some other natives may have to face financial losses, bad reputation and court cases through their professional sphere, by virtue of such malefic retrograde Venus in the fifth house of their horoscopes. If there are some other malefic influences present in the horoscope of a native suffering from this malefic influence, he may have to suffer serious consequences related to the sphere of his profession, reputation or health.

Retrograde Venus in 6th House

Benefic retrograde Venus placed in the sixth house of a horoscope can bless the native with good results related to his marriage, profession, education, health and many other spheres. Accordingly many natives benefitting from this positive placement may witness these good results in different spheres of their lives where the type and quantum of these results may be different in case of different natives, depending on the type and strength of this benefic influence, as well as depending on the overall tone of the horoscopes of these natives. Such benefic influence can give good or very good results related to the professional sphere of the native under its influence and hence, some natives under this effect may achieve success through a wide variety of professions.

Benefic retrograde Venus in the sixth house of a horoscope can bless the native with success through the field of medicals due to which some natives benefitting from this influence may wish to pursue their higher studies in the field of medicals. If there are some other benefic influences present in the horoscopes of these natives, they may complete their studies in the field of medicals and they may become doctors, medical attendants, chemists, nurses and many other people dealing in medical profession, depending on their overall horoscopes. For example, the presence of benefic retrograde Venus and benefic Moon in the sixth house of a horoscope in the sign of Libra can make the native engage in a profession related to medical field and accordingly the native may have his own chemist shop which sells medicines to the people in need, or he may deal in some other type of shop or showroom which sells other necessary medical equipments to the people in need of them.

At the same time, if benefic Mercury is placed in the tent house of this horoscope in the sign of Aquarius, the native under the combined effect of these three benefic planets may achieve even more success through such profession and accordingly, he may become the owner of a big medical showroom which may not only directly sell medicines to needy people on retails basis, but which may also supply some medicines to small medical shops on distribution basis. The native under the combined effect of such benefic retrograde Venus, Moon and Mercury in various houses of his horoscope may start from a small medical shop but he may soon experience good financial incomes, growth and expansion due to which, he may be able to expand his business to a big or very big medical shop or showroom. The presence of benefic Sun in the tenth house of the same horoscope in the sign of Aquarius can supply even more positivity to this equation and accordingly the native under the combined effect of these benefic planets may either own more than one big medical shop or he may become an exclusive distributor for some specific medicines and for a specific region.

At the same time, if benefic Saturn is placed in the eighth house of this horoscope in the sign of Sagittarius, the native under the combined influence of such benefic retrograde Venus and other benefic planets may become the owner of a medical firm or pharmacy. It means that this native may become the manufacturer of many medicines which are made by his company and he may earn very good amount of money through such company. If benefic Rahu also joins benefic Saturn in the eighth house of the same horoscope in the sign of Sagittarius, the native under the combined influence of all these benefic planets may witness great amount of success through his medical firm. This native may become the exclusive manufacturer of some special types of medicines for some period of time and he may earn huge profits through such exclusive rights to such medicines. The medical firm owned by such native may not only make big profits by supplying medicines in his own country, but some of the medicines manufactured by his firm may even sell abroad in good quantities.

Some other natives benefitting from this benefic placement may get engaged in different roles in the same medical field and they may pursue their careers as doctors specializing in various fields, depending on the type and strength of this horoscope, as well as depending on the overall tone of their horoscopes. For example, the presence of benefic retrograde Venus in the sixth house of a horoscope in the sign of Cancer can make the native interested in pursuing his higher studies in some field related to medicals and if benefic Sun is also placed in the sixth house of this horoscope in the sign of Cancer, the native under the combined effect of these benefic planets may complete his studies in medical field and he may start practicing as a professional doctor. At the same time, if benefic Saturn is placed in the eighth house of this horoscope in the sign of Virgo, the success achieved by this native may increase and accordingly he may become an even more successful doctor.

The presence of benefic Mercury in the first house of the same horoscope in the sign of Aquarius can make this equation more positive and accordingly the native may witness better results. Such native under the combined effect of benefic retrograde Venus and Moon in the sixth house, benefic Saturn in the eighth house and benefic Mercury in the first house of his horoscope may become a well recognized and successful doctor and he may earn very good money as well as fame as a doctor. If benefic Mars is placed in the twelfth house of the same horoscope in the sign of Capricorn, the results witnessed by this native may enhance a lot as the presence of benefic as well as exalted Mars in the twelfth house his horoscope can add much more positive energy to this equation. Accordingly the native benefitting from the combined effect of all these benefic influences may start his own hospital after practicing as a doctor in some other hospitals for some time, and he may witness very good amount of success through such hospital. As more positive influences keep adding to this equation, the native under the combined effect of such benefic planets may achieve even more success, recognition and fame through this profession.

Some natives under this benefic influence may become teachers, coaches and trainers of different types depending on the type and strength of this benefic placement, as well as depending on the overall tone of their horoscopes. For example, the presence of benefic retrograde Venus in the sixth house of a horoscope in the sign of Virgo can make the native engage in a profession related to some type of coaching or training and if there are other benefic influences present in his horoscope which support one such profession, the native may witness good results through this profession. For instance, the presence of benefic Saturn in the sixth house of the same horoscope along with benefic retrograde Venus can make the native become a coach or trainer who provides guidance related to personality development, enhancement of leadership abilities and other such subjects.

If at the same time, benefic Sun is placed in the ninth house of this horoscope in the sign of Sagittarius, the native under the combined effect of all these benefic planets may achieve even more success and he may earn more money through this profession. The presence of benefic Mars in the ninth house of the same horoscope in the sign of Sagittarius along with benefic Sun can further improve this equation and the native under the combined effect of all these benefic planets may earn recognition, fame and success along with earning very good amount of money through one such profession. The presence of benefic Mercury in the ninth or tenth house of the same horoscope can further improve this equation and accordingly the native may witness even more success.

The native under the combined effect of such benefic retrograde Venus and benefic Saturn in the sixth house of his horoscope, benefic Sun and benefic Mars in the ninth house and benefic Mercury in the tenth house of his horoscope may also write some books on his field of expertise and he may earn very good amount of financial profits as well as fame and recognition through his books. If benefic Moon or benefic Rahu is also present in the tenth house of this horoscope in the sign of Capricorn along with benefic Mercury, the equation may become even better. Accordingly the native under the combined effect of all these benefic planets in various houses of his horoscope may earn profits and fame not only on national level, but on international level also and he may also receive some formal award for one or more than one of his books. As more positive planets keep adding to this equation, the success achieved by this native may increase more and more.

Benefic retrograde Venus placed in the sixth house of a horoscope can also bless the native with a post of power and authority in some government department and accordingly some natives under this benefic influence may witness this type of results also. For example, the presence of benefic retrograde Venus in the sixth house of a horoscope in the sign of Leo can make the native interested in becoming a police officer or an administrative officer and accordingly the native may try to get a job in one of these departments. If benefic Sun and benefic Mercury are also present in the sixth house of this horoscope in the sign of Leo along with benefic retrograde Venus, the native under the combined influence of these benefic planets may get selected as an administrative officer in some department of government and he may make a good living and status through such job.

However if a combination of benefic retrograde Venus and benefic Mars is present in the sixth house of a horoscope in the sign of Leo, the native under the combined effect of these two benefic planets may be more interested in joining police force, than administrative services. Hence this native may get selected a police officer though he may not directly get selected for a very high or for the highest directly possible rank, as this benefic combination alone may not be capable of doing that. If a combination of benefic Sun and benefic Mercury is present in the tenth house of this horoscope in the sign of Sagittarius when a combination of benefic retrograde Venus and benefic Mars is present in the sixth house of this horoscope in the sign of Leo, the native under the combined influence of these benefic planets may directly get selected at a high or very high rank in police service. Such native may experience a very good career filled with achievements and accomplishments, by virtue of all these benefic planets.

At the same time, if benefic Jupiter is also present in the tenth house of this horoscope in the sign of Sagittarius along with benefic Sun and Mercury when benefic retrograde Venus and benefic Mars are present in the sixth house of the same horoscope, the native under the combined effect of these benefic planets may get selected for the highest possible direct rank in police service. If benefic Rahu is present in the ninth house of this horoscope in the sign of Scorpio or if benefic Moon is present in the tenth house of this horoscope in the sign of Sagittarius, the native under the combined effect of all these benefic planets may have an extraordinary career and he may accomplish great things during his career. Such native is also likely to reach to the very top level of his department, which means that he is likely to work as chief of police of a state before getting retired from his service. If benefic Saturn is placed in the fifth or eight house of this horoscope, the native may receive many formal awards and medals for his exceptional services to his department.

Apart from this, benefic retrograde Venus placed in sixth house of a horoscope can bless the native with success through many other professional spheres and accordingly different natives benefitting from this placement may become successful as different professionals like astrologers, numerologists, doctors, lawyers, consultants, politicians, stock market professionals, teachers, defense professionals, judges, bankers and other professionals working for various professional institutes, software developers, Information and technology professionals, gym trainers, gym owners, yoga instructors, engineers, real estate professionals, diplomats, ministers and many other types of professionals dealing in many other types of professional fields.

On the other hand, the presence of malefic retrograde Venus in the sixth house of a horoscope can trouble the native in many spheres of his life and accordingly the natives suffering from this malefic influence may face problems related to their marriage, children, profession, finances, health and many other spheres of their lives. Once again, the bad results experienced by different natives under this malefic influence may be different in type as well as in quantum, depending on the type and strength of this malefic influence as well as depending on the overall tone of the horoscopes of these natives. Some natives under this malefic influence may have to suffer on account of their professional problems which may be of different types depending on their overall horoscopes.

For example, the presence of malefic retrograde Venus in the sixth house of a horoscope in the sign of Taurus can trouble the native with problems related to his professional sphere and accordingly such native may not be able to establish himself professionally till late or very late in his life. At the same time, if a combination of malefic Mercury and malefic Sun is present in the eighth house of the same horoscope in the sign of Cancer, the combined effect of these malefic influences may add more negativity to this equation and the native may have to suffer much more. Such native may not experience good or solid professional results till late or very late in his life, he may have to work for low paying jobs or even for the jobs belonging to labor category and he may have to remain jobless every now and then, many times in his life.

At the same time, if a combination of malefic Ketu and Jupiter is present in the twelfth house of this horoscope in the sign of Scorpio, the native under the combined influence of these malefic planets may not get a stable profession at all, throughout his life, provided this fact is not challenged by some other benefic influences in his horoscope. Such native may also have to remain jobless almost for his entire life or for a continuous period of many years and he may only be able to get some jobs for some months, after every few years. However, if a combination of benefic Mars and benefic Saturn is placed in the tenth or eleventh house of the same horoscope, the native may experience better results and he may get new jobs soon after losing the old ones, though he may still keep losing jobs under the effect of these malefic planets.

Malefic retrograde Venus in the sixth house of a horoscope can also trouble the native on account of health issues and accordingly some natives suffering from his malefic influence may face various health issues depending on their overall horoscopes. For example, the presence of malefic retrograde Venus in the sixth house of a horoscope in the sign of Taurus can trouble the native with health related problems, though this placement alone may not be sufficient when it comes to trouble the native with some serious type of problems. However, if malefic Mars is also present in the sixth house of the same horoscope in the sign of Taurus, the equation may become much more negative and accordingly the native may suffer more. The native under the combined effect of these malefic planets in the sixth house of his horoscope may suffer from some serious type of health issues or diseases which may trouble him a lot, for a long period of time, or for his entire life.

If at the same time, malefic Ketu is placed in the second house of the same horoscope in the sign of Capricorn, the native under the combined influence of such malefic retrograde Venus, Mars and Ketu may have to suffer from even more serious type of disease or diseases and he may have to undergo surgeries in order to get rid of such diseases, more than once in his life. Moving on, if instead of malefic Ketu, a combination of malefic Ketu and Jupiter is placed in the second house of the same horoscope, the equation can become very negative and it may pose a potential threat to the life of the native under its influence. This is due to the reason that Jupiter which is the lord of ascendant for this horoscope, may not only become very weak in the second house of this horoscope by virtue of its placement in its sign of debilitation which is Capricorn, but it may also get seriously afflicted by such malefic Ketu present in the same house of this horoscope.

Hence the native under the combined effect of these malefic influences may get afflicted by a life threatening disease and if there are no other planets in the horoscope of this native which can act as life savers, the native may have to face much pain, multiple surgeries or other such treatments for this disease, and this disease may still claim his life in the end. Speaking about such benefic life saving influences, the presence of a combination of benefic Sun and benefic Mercury in the first house of this horoscope can still save the life of this native. The native under the combined effect of such malefic combinations of malefic Venus and Mars as well as malefic Ketu and Jupiter in sixth and second house of his horoscope respectively may have to undergo multiple surgeries in order to get rid of a very serious and life threatening disease, but he may finally be able to get out of it, due to the combined effect of such benefic Sun and Mercury in the first house of his horoscope.

Some female natives under this malefic influence may face problems related to their reproductive systems due to which they may have to go through medical treatments as well as complications in order to conceive and deliver children, and they may also have to face serious health issues or diseases due to such malefic influence. For example, the presence of malefic retrograde Venus in the sixth house of a horoscope in the sign of Scorpio can trouble such female native on account of problems related to her reproductive system and accordingly she may have to face delay or medical complications whenever she wants to conceive a child. At the same time, if malefic Saturn, malefic Mars or malefic Ketu is present in the fifth house of the same horoscope in the sign of Libra, the female native under the combined effect of these malefic planets may have to face serious problems related to her reproductive system and she may also have to face abortion of one or more than one of her children, apart from facing long delays.

If malefic retrograde Venus is placed in the sixth house of a horoscope in the sign of Scorpio along with malefic Saturn and malefic Ketu is placed in the fifth house of the same horoscope in the sign of Libra, the female native under the combined effect of all these malefic planets may not be able to deliver a living child throughout her life, though she may experience an abortion or the birth of a dead child, unless there is some other benefic combination in her horoscope, which can promote childbirth. For instance, the presence of a combination of benefic Jupiter and benefic Moon in the second house of the same horoscope can still bless this female native with one or even more than one child, after some complications and medical treatments, despite the presence of all these malefic planets in her horoscope.

Retrograde Venus in 7th House

When working positively, retrograde Venus placed in the seventh house of a horoscope can bless the native with a wide variety of benefits, comforts and pleasures related to the spheres of his marriage, profession, health, finances and many other spheres of his life. Accordingly different natives benefitting from this positive influence may experience good results related to different spheres of their lives which may vary in type and quantum, depending on the type and strength of this influence as well as depending on the overall tone of the horoscopes of these natives. Since seventh house of a horoscope primarily deals with marriage and married life of the native, the presence of such benefic influence in the seventh house of a horoscope can especially bless the native with a good and gainful marriage due to which different natives benefitting from this positive influence may witness different types of gains through their marriages depending on their overall horoscopes.

Some natives under the effect of this benefic influence may get married to someone belonging to a foreign country which has a higher or much higher standard of living than their own country and they may settle in that foreign country on the basis of that marriage, thereby seeing very good rise in their overall living standard as well as in their profession. For example, the presence of benefic retrograde Venus in the seventh house of a horoscope in the sign of Libra can bless the native with a beautiful and caring wife who may belong to a foreign country of higher living standard, though this placement alone may not promise a wife from a foreign country. However if benefic

Rahu is placed in the seventh house of the same horoscope in the sign of Libra along with benefic Venus, and benefic Mars is placed in the twelfth house of this horoscope in the sign of Pisces, the native may certainly get married to a beautiful wife hailing from a foreign country with a higher standard of living.

The combined effect of these three benefic planets in the seventh and twelfth house of the horoscope of this native can not only bless him with a beautiful wife from a foreign country, but the same benefic effect can also get the native settled in that foreign country. Such native may earn good amount of money in that foreign country and he may also enjoy a far better quality of life by virtue of his settlement in that foreign country due to his marriage. If benefic Saturn is placed in the tenth house of this horoscope in the sign of Capricorn, the native under the combined effect of such benefic retrograde Venus, Rahu, Mars and Saturn may get married to a woman who is elder to him in age or who has already been divorced once, but who at the same time is beautiful, caring and richer or much richer than native.

The fortune of this native may change overnight by virtue of this marriage, as he may not only get a beautiful wife and settle in a foreign country with a higher standard of living, but he may also become rich by virtue of his marriage to such woman. If benefic Moon is placed in the second house of this horoscope in the sign of Taurus, the native under the combined influence of such benefic retrograde Venus and other benefic planets mentioned in this example may profit even more. The wife of such native may either make him a partner in her already well established business or she may give him a big amount of money to start some business of his own due to which, the native may become professionally well established soon after his marriage to such female.

Looking at these two possibilities, if benefic Sun is placed in the fourth house of this horoscope in the sign of Cancer or if benefic Sun is placed in the eighth house of this horoscope in the sign of Scorpio, the native is more likely to get a partnership in the already established business of her wife. On the other hand, if benefic Sun is placed in the sign of Leo in the fifth house of this horoscope when benefic retrograde Venus and benefic Rahu are placed in the seventh house, benefic Mars is placed in the twelfth house and benefic Moon is placed in the second house of the same horoscope, the native under the combined effect of these benefic planets is more likely to get a big financial support from her wife and start his own business. However, in both the cases, the native may profit a lot in the sphere of his profession and overall finances, by virtue of such marriage to a beautiful women belonging to a foreign country.

Some other natives profiting from this benefic influence may get married to rich and well established people and some of them may get married to a person belonging to a family which holds some type of power and authority due to which, these native may witness rise in their social status as well as in their authority, depending on their overall horoscopes. For example, the presence of benefic retrograde Venus in the seventh house of a horoscope in the sign of Taurus can bless the native with a beautiful and well mannered wife in case of male natives, whereas the same benefic placement in case of female natives can bless them with a well established, rich or a powerful husband.

Following the case of female natives this time, if benefic retrograde Venus is placed in the seventh house of a horoscope in the sign of Taurus and a combination of benefic Jupiter and benefic Rahu is placed in the eleventh house of the same horoscope in the sign of Gemini, the female native under the combined influence of these benefic planets may get married to a rich or a very rich person and she may enjoy a fair share of his money and resources after her marriage. If benefic Sun or benefic Mars is placed in the eighth house of the same horoscope, let's say benefic Sun is present in the eighth house of the same horoscope in the sign of Gemini, the native under the combined effect of these four benefic planets may get a husband who is not only rich but who also belongs to a family that holds some political or other type of power and authority. Hence the female native in this case may witness a very good rise not only in her financial equation and quality of living, but she may also witness a very good rise in her social status and authority also.

Moving on, if benefic Mars is placed in the tenth house of this horoscope in the sign of Leo, the female native under the combined effect of such benefic retrograde Venus, Jupiter, Rahu, Sun and Mars in various houses of her horoscope may not only get married to a man belonging to a very well established political family or even to a man belonging to a royal family, but she may also enjoy a very good amount of personal authority by virtue of such marriage. It means that such native may herself get elevated to a post of power and authority by virtue of her marriage to such man or she may deal with a large number of people on daily basis by virtue of being a member of this family and she may make a good name for herself through the process.

At the same time, if benefic Saturn is placed in the fourth house of this horoscope in the sign of Capricorn, benefic Moon is placed in the seventh house of this horoscope in the sign of Taurus along with benefic retrograde Venus and benefic Mercury is placed in the ninth house of this horoscope in the sign of Cancer, the female native under the combined influence of all these benefic planets may come across some of the most wonderful results that a female can ever experience through her marriage. The female native under the combined effect of all these benefic planets in various houses of her horoscope may get married to a man who belongs to the one of the richest, one of the politically most established or one of the most royal families of his country. Hence this female native may witness a great rise not only in her standard of living, but in her overall status, authority, fame, recognition and respect that she gains through common people, in a short period of time after her marriage.

The same combination of all these benefic planets in the horoscope of this female native including benefic retrograde Venus in the seventh house of her horoscope is not only capable of blessing her with all the above mentioned results through her marriage but it is capable of blessing her with even more. If the other factors in her horoscope are favorable, such female native may become the queen or head of state of an entire country by virtue of her marriage in one such royal or political family. It should be noted that though the placement of all the planets in the horoscope of this female has been mentioned, I have still used the term 'if her horoscope is favorable'. This is due to the fact that though planetary placements in various houses, signs and in various combinations is one of the most important aspects in a horoscope, it is not everything and more is required, particularly when extreme types of results whether good or bad are considered.

Explaining this example in more details, if the combination of benefic retrograde Venus and benefic Moon is placed in the seventh house of this horoscope in the sign of Taurus as well as in the nakshatra of Rohini, benefic Jupiter is placed in the eleventh house of this horoscope in the sign of Virgo as well as in the nakshatra of UttraPhalguni, benefic Mercury is placed in the ninth house of this horoscope in the sign of Cancer as well as in the nakshatra of Pushya or in the nakshatra of

Ashlesha, benefic Mars is placed in the tenth house of this horoscope in the sign of Leo as well as in the nakshtra of Magha or UttraPhalguni and the ascendant is rising in the sign of Scorpio as well as in the nakshatra of Jyeshtha, the female native under the combined influence of these combinations has much better chances of becoming a queen or head of the state of a country.

However, if some of these combinations change like the ascendant rises in the nakshatra of Anuradha, benefic Moon and benefic retrograde Venus are placed in the nakshatra of Mrigshira and benefic Mars is placed in the nakshatra of PurvaPhalguni, the results may change. Accordingly this female native may not be able to become the queen of a country or head of state of a country though she may get very close to this title, once or more than once in her life. Looking at some other factors, if all the planetary combinations are favorable in terms of houses, signs as well as in terms of nakshatras as already described, and a planetary main period of Moon, Mars or Venus hits this female native at a relevant age which is between any age above the age of 35 or 42, she may achieve one of these titles.

On the other hand, if a planetary period of Rahu or Saturn is in effect when such an opportunity presents itself, the same female native may not be able to achieve one of these titles, though she may definitely get something else which is of somewhat less value than one of these things. For example, she may be offered the post of party president of the ruling party in a country and she may also be offered a number of other financial as well as other benefits instead of being offered the post of the head of that country. Similarly she may get a special post of honor which comes with a number of benefits as well as with great respect and authority, instead of becoming the ruling queen of a country. Astrology is full of possibilities as there are billions of possible combinations in a horoscope and accordingly, there are billions of possible good or bad things that can happen to a native under the influence of such different combinations.

Apart from this, benefic retrograde Venus placed in the seventh house of a horoscope can not only bless the native with many other types of good results through his marriage, but it can also bless him with good results related to his profession, finances, health, reputation and many other spheres of his life, depending on his overall horoscope. On the other hand, retrograde Venus placed in the seventh house of a horoscope can trouble the native with a wide variety of problems related to his marriage, profession, financial equation, health, reputation and many other spheres of his life, if it turns negative in a horoscope. Accordingly many natives suffering from this malefic influence may have to witness bad results related to many spheres of their lives where such bad results can be different in type and in quantum for different natives, depending on the type and strength of this malefic placement, as well as depending on the overall tone of the horoscopes of these natives.

As seventh house of a horoscope primarily deals with marriage aspect of the native, such malefic influence can cause many problems and troubles in the marriage and married life of the native, depending on the overall tone of the horoscope of the native in question. For example, the presence of malefic retrograde Venus in the seventh house of a horoscope in the sign of Aries can not only cause delay in the marriage of the native under its influence, but it can also cause disturbances in the marriage of such native. Accordingly the native under the effect of this malefic influence may have to wait till late or very late in order to get married, depending on his overall horoscope. Once married, the native under the effect of this malefic influence may have to face issues related to lack of trust, lack of compatibility and lack of understanding with his life partner and these issues can intensify if there are other negative planets in the horoscope of this native which support such disturbances.

For instance, the presence of malefic Mars in the second house of the same horoscope in the sign of Scorpio can add more negativity to this equation, particularly if Mars placed in the second house of this horoscope forms Manglik Dosh in the horoscope. Accordingly the native under the combined effect of such malefic retrograde Venus and Manglik Dosh may have to face serious problems in his marriage. The wife of such native may give him very hard time as she may be very aggressive and doubting by nature and hence she may keep arguing and fighting with the native on account of one thing or the other. If malefic Rahu or malefic Ketu is placed in the seventh house of the same horoscope in the sign of Aries or if one of them is present in the second house of the same horoscope in the sign of Scorpio, the equation may become even more negative. Accordingly the native under the combined effect of all these malefic influences may have to face one or more than one broken marriage and even the divorces may finalize after much drama and trouble.

Some other natives under the effect of this malefic influence may have to face delay in their marriage and they may be able to get married late or very late in their lives depending on their overall horoscopes. For example, the presence of malefic retrograde Venus in the seventh house of a horoscope in the sign of Aquarius can delay the marriage and accordingly the native may have to wait till late in his life in order to get married. Such malefic placement can also trouble the native on account of some marriage proposals which may come closer to being finalized but which may not materialize in the end. If malefic

Ketu is placed in the second house of the same horoscope in the sign of Virgo or if malefic Saturn is placed in the twelfth house of the same horoscope in the sign of Cancer, the native under the combined effect of these malefic influences may not be able to get married till 35 years of his age or even till 41 years of his age, if there is no other planetary combination present in the horoscope of this native, which promotes a timely marriage.

Considering one more possibility in the same example, if malefic retrograde Venus is placed in the seventh house of a horoscope in the sign of Aquarius, a combination of malefic Ketu and malefic Saturn is present in the second house of this horoscope in the sign of Virgo and malefic Jupiter is placed in the sixth house of the same horoscope in the sign of Capricorn, the native under the combined effect of all these malefic planets may not get married at all, and he may have to remain single throughout his life. Even if there is some other planetary combination present in the horoscope of this native, which is benefic and which promotes marriage, such marriage may not last long and the native may have to remain single for his life, after the divorce is finalized in such marriage.

Apart from this, malefic retrograde Venus placed in the seventh house of a horoscope can trouble the native in many other ways through his marriage and accordingly many natives suffering from this malefic influence may have to face many other types of problems and troubles through their marriages, depending on their overall horoscopes. Malefic retrograde Venus in the seventh house of a horoscope can also trouble the native with problems related to his profession, overall finances, reputation, health and many other things. Such malefic placement can especially prove very bad for the health and longevity of the native and accordingly some natives under the effect of this malefic influence may have to suffer from serious diseases. In an extreme case of this type, the native under the combined effect of such malefic retrograde Venus in the seventh house of his horoscope and some other negative planets in his horoscope may get afflicted by a life threatening disease which may claim his life at a relatively young or very young age.

Retrograde Venus in 8th House

Benefic retrograde Venus placed in the eighth house of a horoscope can bless the native with good results related to his marriage, profession, overall health, finances, wisdom, spiritual growth and many other good things. Accordingly many natives benefitting from this benefic influence may witness good results related to some of these spheres of their lives where the type and quantum of results witnessed by different natives under such benefic influence may be different, depending on the type and strength of this benefic placement as well as depending on the overall tone of the horoscopes of these natives. Some natives under the effect of this good influence may witness good or very good amount of success through various professional spheres as this benefic influence is capable of blessing the native with success through various types of professions.

For example, the presence of benefic retrograde Venus in the eighth house of a horoscope in the sign of Pisces can render certain special abilities to the native under its influence and accordingly the native may have a much deeper insight and understanding of many aspects of nature and the working of universe, which are not easy for other people to understand. Hence the native gifted by such abilities may pursue a field of profession as well as course of life, which deals with one of these spheres through which the native may guide and help other people understand these secrets in a better way, or he may deal with healing other people through some type of special knowledge or talent that he may have. Such native may have interest in the study of astrology, numerology, Ayurveda, healing techniques of meditation, yoga for transformation of body and mind, chanting of specific mantras or engaging in specific procedures which can benefit people, tantra, spiritualism or some other field which is similar to these fields.

However this benefic placement alone may not be capable of blessing the native with a career in one of these fields and more support may be required from other parts of his horoscope. If benefic Sun is also present in the eighth house of the same horoscope in the sign of Pisces along with benefic retrograde Venus, the native under the combined effect of these benefic planets may adopt one of the already mentioned spheres as his full time profession and he may achieve good amount of success through such field. If benefic Rahu is placed in the fourth house of this horoscope in the sign of Scorpio and benefic Mercury is placed in the ninth house of this horoscope in the sign of Aries, the native under the combined effect of all these benefic planets may become an astrologer and he may achieve very good amount of success through this profession. Such native may also earn fame and recognition through his profession and the results witnessed by him may improve further, if some other benefic influences are present in his horoscope, which support success through this profession.

For instance, the presence of benefic Jupiter in the ninth house of this horoscope in the sign of Aries along with benefic Mercury can increase the success achieved by this native and accordingly the native under the combined effect of these benefic planets may become even more famous as well as more successful, and he may also appear on some television shows related to astrology. The presence of a combination of benefic Moon and benefic Mars in the tenth house of this horoscope in the sign of Taurus can further improve this equation and accordingly the native under the combined effect of all these benefic planets including benefic retrograde Venus in the eighth house of his horoscope may witness great amount of success and fame as an astrologer. Such native may not only become successful and famous on national level, but he may also become known on international level. If benefic Jupiter is placed in the first, fourth, fifth, tenth or twelfth house of this horoscope, the results achieved by the native may become even better.

Looking at another possible profession in the same example, if benefic retrograde Venus is placed in the eighth house of a horoscope in the sign of Pisces and benefic Moon is either placed in the first house of this horoscope in the sign of Leo or it is present in the tenth house of this horoscope in the sign of Taurus, the native under the combined effect of these benefic planets may choose the path of spiritualism instead of choosing a line like astrology. Such native may conduct studies and researches directly related to the field of spiritual growth of the soul and he may start teaching or training other people on how to achieve more and more spiritual growth, after his age of 35 years.

If benefic retrograde Venus is placed in the eighth house of a horoscope in the sign of Pisces, benefic Moon is placed in the first house of the same horoscope in the sign of Leo and a combination of benefic Sun and benefic Mercury is placed in the ninth house of the same horoscope in the sign of Aries, the native under the combined effect of all these benefic plants may witness good results of much higher quantum. Such native may either become the head of a big branch of a well established spiritual organization or he may start his own spiritual mission which teaches and trains people how to achieve more and more spiritual growth. If benefic Jupiter is present in the first house of this horoscope in the sign of Leo along with benefic Moon, the success achieve by this native may increase and accordingly the native under the combined effect of these benefic influences may become a well known spiritual guru who may also render the teachings of religion.

The presence of benefic Rahu in the tenth house of this horoscope in the sign of Taurus can further improve this equation due to which the native under the combined effect of these benefic influences may achieve success and fame as a spiritual as well as religious guru, not only on the national level, but on the international level also. Such native may have a large number of devotees who follow him, respect and worship him. At the same time, if benefic Saturn is also present in the tenth house of the same horoscope in the sign of Taurus along with benefic Rahu, the native under the combined effect of all these benefic planets including benefic retrograde Venus in the eighth house of his horoscope may achieve phenomenal amount of success as a spiritual and religious guru. Such native may appear on a large number of television shows and he may also write many books on the field of his expertise.

Benefic retrograde Venus in eighth house of a horoscope can also bless the native with a post of power and authority in some government department and accordingly some natives under the effect of this benefic influence may become officers with different departments of government, depending on the type and strength of this benefic influence as well as depending on the overall tone of their horoscopes. For example, the presence of benefic retrograde Venus in the eighth house of a horoscope in the sign of Scorpio can bless the native under its influence with a good post in some financial department of government like in a government owned bank, some revenue department or in any other such department which deals with finances or revenue of some kind. On the other hand, the presence of benefic retrograde Venus in the eighth house of a horoscope in the sign of Aries along with benefic Mercury can bless the native with a post of authority in police force or the same combination can bless the native with the post of a judge in some court of law, depending on his overall horoscope.

Moving on, the presence of benefic retrograde Venus in the eight house of a horoscope in the sign of Leo along with along with benefic Mars can bless the native with the post of an administrative officer if his overall horoscope allows it whereas the presence of benefic retrograde Venus in the eighth house of a horoscope in the sign of Aquarius along with benefic Mars can make the native become a doctor in some government department, if his overall horoscope allows it. Likewise, the presence of benefic retrograde Venus in the eighth house of a horoscope in the sign of Libra along with benefic Saturn when benefic Jupiter is placed in the tenth house of the same horoscope can bless the native with the post of an officer who represents his country in some office, embassy or high commission opened by the government of his country, in some foreign country, if the overall horoscope is supportive. The number of ways and professional fields through which this benefic influence can bless a native are countless and the example mentioned here are just a few of them.

Some natives under the benefic influence of this placement can also excel in the field of some type of research and analysis and they can achieve good or very good amount of success through such field, depending on their overall horoscopes. For example, the presence of benefic retrograde Venus in the eighth house of a horoscope in the sign of Pisces can make the native more and more interested in science as well as in scientific researches and discoveries. If benefic Mars is also present in the eighth house of the same horoscope in the sign of Pisces, the native under the combined effect of these benefic planets may actually become a scientist after completing his study in some subject of science on a very high level, and he may start engaging in researches related to his subject in science. If a combination of benefic Jupiter and benefic Saturn is placed in the first house of this horoscope in the sign of Leo, the native under the combined influence of these benefic planets may become more successful as a scientist and he may discover or invent something new that comes under his field of expertise.

It means that such native may become an inventor and he may invent or discover some new theory, phenomenon, formula or device which may add much credit and recognition to his name. If benefic Mercury is placed in the second house of this horoscope in the sign of Virgo and benefic Rahu is placed in the tenth house of this horoscope in the sign of Taurus, the native under the combined influence of such benefic retrograde Venus and all other benefic planets mentioned in this example may earn very good amount of success, fame, recognition as well as money by virtue of some invention made by him. Such native under the combined effect of these benefic planets may also receive some formal award of high or very high honor, by virtue of such invention made by him, provided his overall horoscope allows it. Apart from this, benefic retrograde Venus in the eighth house of a horoscope can bless the native with success through many other professional spheres also and such benefic placement can also bless the native with good results related to his marriage, finances, overall health and lifespan, among many other good things.

On the other hand, malefic retrograde Venus placed in the eighth house of a horoscope can trouble the native on many fronts of his life including his marriage, profession and health due to which many natives suffering from this malefic influence may feel the heat of this placement in some of these spheres of their lives. Here again, the type and intensity of the problems faced by different natives under this malefic influence may be different depending on the type and strength of this malefic influence, as well as depending on the overall tone of the horoscopes of these natives. Some natives under the effect of this malefic influence may have to face problems in their marriages which may depend on their overall horoscopes. For example, the presence of malefic retrograde Venus in the eighth house of a horoscope in the sign of Aries may not delay the marriage of the native under its influence but it may cause a number of problems depending on the overall horoscope of the native.

The native under the effect of such malefic influence may get married to a women suffering from a serious health disease which may even be fatal in extreme cases, and the native may not know about this disease before his marriage. It means that either such disease is known to his wife as well as her family but they intentionally hide it from the native in order to get her married to the native or such disease may become visible some years after the marriage of this native. The native may not be able to enjoy his marriage properly due to such disease of his wife and he may have to suffer a lot on the front of expenses, mental tension and physical tension by virtue of such disease of her wife.

If malefic Jupiter is placed in the third house of the same horoscope in the sign of Scorpio, malefic Ketu is placed in the second house of this horoscope in the sign of Libra and malefic Rahu is placed in the eighth house of this horoscope in the sign of Aries along with malefic retrograde Venus, the native under the combined effect of all these malefic planets may have to lose his wife to such disease. Hence the wife of this native may die because of such fatal disease which may trouble her as well as the native for many years and which may also make the native spend very big amount of money towards the treatment of such disease. If there are no other benefic planets in the horoscope of this native, which show good results related to marriage and if there are some other malefic planets which cause problems in the marriage of the native, the native under the combined effect of all these malefic planets may have to lose more than one wife to diseases or accidents.

Considering another type of example, the presence of malefic retrograde Venus in the eighth house of a horoscope in the sign of Sagittarius may once again not delay the marriage of a native, but it may cause different type of problems for this native. This type of malefic influence may be especially very bad for female natives and accordingly the female natives suffering from this malefic influence may have to face more troubles than the male native under the same malefic influence. A female under the effect of this malefic influence may get married to a man who may not only be a criminal or a bad person of some other type like he may be addicted to liquor or he may be a drug addict or a gambler, but who may also trouble this native a lot through by virtue of these vices.

For instance, if malefic Rahu is also placed in the eighth house of the same horoscope in the sign of Sagittarius along with malefic retrograde Venus, the husband of such female native may be a criminal or a gambler depending on his overall horoscope and this female native may have to suffer a lot due to such vices of her husband. Her husband may take away or even snatch money from her and he may also abuse her not only verbally but physically also, from time to time, which means that such female native may have to suffer from a very poor quality of marriage, unless there are some other benefic planets in her horoscope which promote a good marriage.

However, if instead of malefic Rahu, malefic Mars is placed in the eighth house of this horoscope in the sign of Sagittarius along with malefic retrograde Venus, the female native under the combined effect of these malefic planets may have to suffer even more, though in a different way. Such female native may get married to a criminal or an otherwise very bad or selfish type of person and she may have to face verbal abuse and physical violence on routine basis. The husband of such female native may trouble her a lot and she may have to face many other types of problems too, through this marriage. If there are some other malefic influences present in the horoscope of this female like if malefic Jupiter is placed in the twelfth house of this horoscope in the sign of Aries and a combination of malefic Sun and Mercury is placed in the sixth house of this horoscope in the sign of Libra, the female native under the combined effect of all these malefic influences may get murdered by her husband, unless there is some strong life saving planet in her horoscope.

Speaking about such life saving combination, the presence of a combination of benefic Saturn and benefic Moon in the first house of this horoscope in the sign of Taurus can still save the life of this female native and this benefic combination can also improve the quality of her marriage. Accordingly, the female native under the combined effect of all these malefic planets including malefic retrograde Venus in the eighth house of her horoscope and all these benefic planets may have to suffer verbal abuse and physical violence during the initial years of her marriage, but things may become better and better with the passage of time and she witness a much better quality of marriage, after 10 or 15 years of her marriage.

Similarly, the presence of malefic retrograde Venus in the eighth house of a horoscope can trouble the native with many other types of problems which may be related not only to his marriage, but which may also be related to his profession, health, finances, lifespan and many other important spheres of his life. For example, the presence of malefic retrograde Venus in the eighth house of a horoscope in the sign of Virgo can trouble the native on account of problems related to his marriage as well as those related to his profession and such problems in his profession can further intensify if a combination of malefic Ketu and malefic Jupiter is placed in the twelfth house of his horoscope in the sign of Capricorn. Accordingly the native under the combined influence of these malefic planets may not be able to establish professionally till late or very late in his life and he may have to start from a scratch, many times in his life, after losing whatever he had.

Taking another example, the presence of malefic retrograde Venus in the eighth house of horoscope in the sign of Virgo can also trouble the native with problems related to his health and such problems can intensify if malefic Rahu is also present in the eight house of the same horoscope in the sign of Virgo. The native under the combined effect of these malefic planets may get addicted to drugs and he may have to suffer a lot on the front of his health, by virtue of such addiction. If at the same time, malefic Sun is placed in the second house of his horoscope in the sign of Pisces and malefic Mercury is placed in the third house of his horoscope in the sign of Aries, the native under the combined effect of all these malefic planets may die at a relatively young or very young age, due to the overdose of some drug or due to some fatal disease caused by the prolonged use of some drug.

Retrograde Venus in 9th House

When working positively, retrograde Venus placed in the ninth house of a horoscope can bless the native with good results related to marriage, profession, fame, finances, overall health and many other spheres of his life. Accordingly the natives benefitting from this placement may witness such good results where the type and quantum of these good results may be different in case of different natives, depending on the type and strength of this benefic placement, as well as depending on the overall tone of the horoscopes of these natives. Benefic retrograde Venus in the ninth house of a horoscope can render good, very good or great amount of professional success and fame to the native under its influence and accordingly some natives under this influence may achieve success through a range professional spheres, depending on their overall horoscopes.

Some natives benefitting from this benefic influence may excel in some creative fields like acting, directing, singing, writing, dancing, painting or in some other such type of creative field. For example, the presence of benefic retrograde Venus in the ninth house of a horoscope in the sign of Virgo can make the native under its influence interested in acting or in some other type of sphere related to movie making like photography or video making. Accordingly the native may follow one such creative line depending on the overall horoscope and he may also engage in one such line on professional basis, if there are other supportive influences in his horoscope. For instance, if benefic Saturn is placed in the fifth house of this horoscope in the sign of Taurus, the native under the combined effect of these benefic planets may pursue a career as an actor and he may start working as a stage actor, a television actor or a movie actor depending on the other factors in his horoscope.

However it should be noted that the combined effect of these two benefic planets is not capable of blessing the native with much success as an actor because retrograde Venus placed in the ninth house of this horoscope is debilitated and accordingly it may not help the native much when it comes to bless him with practical and materialistic results through acting, though this placement can certainly bless him with equal amount of acting abilities as any other placement of benefic Venus in this house of a horoscope can. Hence such benefic retrograde Venus in the ninth house of this horoscope may bless the native with a very good amount of creative abilities but it may need more strength from some other benefic planets in order to deliver practical results through such creative abilities. Since benefic Saturn is placed in the fifth house of his horoscope, it has no direct interaction with such benefic retrograde Venus placed in the ninth house of the same horoscope and hence this additional strength has to come through some other positive planet.

The best possible positive planet in this case can be benefic Mercury, as Mercury is the lord of Virgo and it is also exalted in Virgo due to which, the presence of benefic Mercury in the sign of Virgo can provide much more strength to such benefic but debilitated Venus and it can also cancel the debilitation status of such benefic retrograde Venus placed in the ninth house of this horoscope. Accordingly, the native under the combined effect of these three benefic planets may witness much more professional success through the field of acting and hence he may become a lead actor in movies. Such native can achieve good amount of success and fame and his success may improve even more, if benefic Sun is also present in the ninth house of the same horoscope in the sign of Virgo. The native under the combined influence of all these benefic planets may achieve very good amount of success as a lead actor and he may also have a large number of people following him.

This equation can improve even more if benefic Mars is also present in the ninth house of the same horoscope in the sign of Virgo as the combination of these four benefic planets in the horoscope of this native can bless him with great amount of success and fame as an actor. Accordingly the native under the combined influence of such benefic retrograde Venus, Mercury, Sun and Mars in the ninth house of his horoscope in the sign of Virgo and benefic Saturn in the fifth house of his horoscope in the sign of Taurus may become a big celebrity, an iconic star or even a superstar depending on the overall tone of his horoscope. It should be noted that the native under the combined influence of all these benefic planets is more likely to become famous as an action movie star, instead of being known as a romantic star or as a comedian.

The presence of benefic Moon in the tenth house of the same house in the sign of Libra however, can add a touch of romance to the overall acting image of this native and accordingly the native under the combined effect of all these benefic planets may receive recognition for some of his romantic performances also, though he is still likely to be primarily known as an action hero. Such native is also likely to receive many formal awards for many of his performances and he is likely to have an exceptional career as an actor. If benefic Jupiter is placed in the seventh house of this horoscope in the sign of Cancer, the presence of such benefic and exalted Jupiter in the seventh house of this horoscope can add much more positive energy to this already positive equation and accordingly the native may witness even better results.

The native under the combined effect of all these benefic planets may become an actor of legendary status and he may not only become famous on national level but he may also become a well known celebrity on international level also. The combined effect of all these benefic planets including benefic retrograde Venus in the ninth house and benefic exalted Jupiter in the seventh house of this horoscope can also make the native a very versatile actor who may not only be known for his action performances, but he may also receive recognition and some formal awards for his acting performances related to the genres of comedy, romance, drama and many other genres of acting. However, this native is still likely to be primarily known as an action star particularly during the early years of his acting career and he may start adding more and more variety to his acting towards the later years of his acting career.

Looking at one more possible option with the same placement of this benefic planet, the presence of benefic retrograde Venus in the ninth house of a horoscope in the sign of Virgo can also render special abilities to the native due to which the native may also shine as a politician, depending on the overall tone of his horoscope. For the readers who may be surprised by the fact how such debilitated retrograded Venus in the ninth house of a horoscope can make the native an actor as well as a politician, let me mention this fact here that good acting abilities, good speech abilities and many other such abilities which can make the native shine as an actor are also required if the native wants to be a successful politician. Some of the politicians are even bigger actors than the ones who are actively pursuing a career in acting and hence this fact should come as no surprise that the same influence which can make a native an actor, can make him a politician. It should be understood that many basic abilities of both such natives which is an actor and a politician are the same or similar, and only the field of their application is different.

Moving on with the topic, though benefic retrograde Venus in the ninth house of a horoscope in the sign of Virgo can also render good political wisdom to the native but this placement alone is once again not sufficient to bless the native with good practical results as a politician. However, if benefic Mercury or benefic Moon is also present in the ninth house of this horoscope in the sign of Virgo, the native under the combined effect of these two benefic planets, let's say benefic retrograde Venus and benefic Mercury can see good results through the field of politics, provided there are some other supporting influences in his horoscope. For instance, if benefic Saturn is placed in the sixth house of this horoscope in the sign of Gemini, the native under the combined effect of all these benefic planets may become a full time politician and he may also achieve good amount of success through this field. Such native is likely to make a slow start in politics and then he is likely to pick up slowly from there, and he may witness better and better results with the passage of time.

It should be noted here how the change in placement of Saturn in these two examples can change the results achieved by the native. In the first example, a combination of benefic retrograde Venus and benefic Mercury is present in the ninth house of this horoscope in the sign of Virgo, and the presence of benefic Saturn in the fifth house of the same horoscope bends the native towards the field of acting. However, in the second example, the combination of benefic retrograde Venus and benefic Mercury remains the same in the ninth house of this horoscope in the sign of Virgo and only a change in the placement of benefic Saturn from fifth house of this horoscope to the sixth house of this horoscope in the sign of Gemini, makes the native more interested in politics. This is why I mention many times that astrology is the science of possibilities and billions of possible combinations may be present in a horoscope due to which the native may witness different types of results, even if one of the factors changes in his horoscope.

Coming back to the present example, if benefic Sun is present in the eight house of this horoscope in the sign of Leo when a combination of benefic retrograde Venus and benefic Mercury is present in the ninth house and benefic Saturn is placed in the sixth house of the same horoscope, the native may achieve even more success through politics. The native under the combined effect of these benefic planets may achieve a post of power and authority through politics and he may also earn good amount of money and fame through this field. At the same time, if a combination of benefic Jupiter and benefic Rahu is present in the tenth house of this horoscope in the sign of Libra, much more positivity may be added to this already positive equation. Accordingly the native under the combined influence of all these benefic planets may become a famous and a very big leader on a state level and he may also become a well known leader on national level.

Such native may get blessed with the post of a minister more than once in his life, by virtue of winning an election and representing his region in the state assembly. The presence of a combination of benefic Moon and benefic Mars in the seventh house of this horoscope in the sign of Cancer can add even more positivity to this equation and the results may become great instead of being very good. Accordingly the native under the combined effect of all these benefic planets including benefic retrograde Venus and benefic Mercury in the ninth house of his horoscope in the sign of Virgo may witness success on national level and he may become a very big political leader of national fame. It should be noted that though Mars is debilitated in the sign of Cancer, the presence of benefic Moon in the same sign will cancel its debilitation status and since the overall horoscope of the native is already very strong and such benefic Chandra Mangal Yoga is being formed in a Kendra house of this horoscope, NeechBhanga RajYoga will be formed in the horoscope of this native in this case.

Accordingly the native under the combined effect of such Neechbhanga RajYoga, Chandra Mangal Yoga, a combination of benefic retrograde Venus and benefic Mercury in the ninth house of his horoscope and all other benefic planets in the already mentioned houses of his horoscope may not only become a very big political leader of national fame, he may also become the head of state of his country. It means that the native blessed by all these benefic planets may become the prime minister or the president of a country, provided his overall horoscope supports it. Even if there are some aspects in the horoscope of this native which don't support such a post of the highest honor and authority, the native under the combined effect of all these benefic planets may still achieve a post of great power and authority which may be second, just to the highest post. It means that the native in this case may get the post of vice president or home minister of a country.

For the readers interested in astrology as well as for the astrologers who think that the presence of debilitated planets in a horoscope can only bring more and more problems for the native, this horoscope is a very good example to learn. Though there are two debilitated planets in this horoscope, the native may still rise to a post of very high authority or even to the post of highest authority, if the overall horoscope supports it. The debilitation status of Mars as well as retrograde Venus is cancelled in this case by virtue of presence of the benefic lords of their signs of debilitations with them and whereas a very good resultant combination may be formed by retrograde

Venus and Mercury, Neechbhanga RajYoga may be formed by the combination of benefic Mars and Moon.

Apart from this, benefic retrograde Venus in the ninth house can bless the native with good results through many other professional spheres and the same benefic influence can also bless the native with good results related to his marriage, education, finances, reputation, health, lifespan and many other spheres of his life. Accordingly the natives benefitting from this benefic influence may witness such good results of different quantum in different fields of their lives, depending on their overall horoscopes. Ninth house of a horoscope is a very important as well as a very resourceful house and accordingly the presence of one or more than one benefic planet can do very good things to the native.

On the other hand, malefic retrograde Venus placed in the ninth house of a horoscope can cause a number of problems for the native under its influence. Accordingly the natives suffering from this malefic influence may have to face problems related to the field of marriage, profession, financial sphere, health, reputation, lifespan or some other sphere of their lives, depending on the type and strength of this malefic influence as well as depending on the overall tone of their horoscopes. Some natives under the effect of this malefic influence may have to face problems related to their marriage due to which some of them may have to wait till late or very late in their lives in order to get married, whereas some other such natives may have to face disturbances and troubles through their marriages.

For example, the presence of malefic retrograde Venus in the ninth house of a horoscope in the sign of Virgo can delay the marriage of the native under its influence and accordingly the native may get married late in his life. At the same time, if malefic Saturn, malefic Mercury or malefic Ketu is placed in the seventh house of the same horoscope in the sign of Leo, the marriage of such native may be delayed further and he may be able to get married only after 35 years of his age or even after his age of 42. However, if a combination of malefic retrograde Venus and Sun is present in the ninth house of this horoscope in the sign of Libra, malefic Saturn is present in the seventh house of this horoscope in the sign of Leo and malefic Rahu is placed in the eighth house of this horoscope in the sign of Virgo, the native under the combined effect of these malefic influences may not get married throughout his life and he may have to remain single forever, unless there is some planet which strongly promotes marriage in the horoscope of such native.

Speaking about such a planet, the presence of benefic Jupiter in the ninth house of the same horoscope in the sign of Libra along with malefic retrograde Venus and Sun can still get the native married with delay, despite the presence of such marriage denying combinations in the horoscope of this native. Accordingly, the native may get married due to such benefic Jupiter, though he may have to wait till 36th or 38th year of his life in order to get married, due to the combined effect of these malefic planets. It should be noted that though the native under the combined effect of these benefic planets may still get married due to the intervention of benefic Jupiter, he may not be able to enjoy a good marriage and he may have to make many compromises in his marriage.

Taking another example, the presence of malefic retrograde Venus in the ninth house of a horoscope in the sign of Sagittarius may not delay the marriage of the native under its impact but the same malefic influence may cause problems after marriage. Accordingly the native may have to face issues related to physical as well as mental compatibility with his wife and such issues can trouble him more and more with the passage of time. If malefic Jupiter is also present in the ninth house of the same horoscope in the sign of Sagittarius along with malefic retrograde Venus, this equation may become even more negative and troublesome. Hence the native under the combined influence of these two malefic planets may get involved in an extramarital affair with some other woman as he may not get much value from his marriage and he may do so after many years of suffering through such marriage.

If malefic Rahu or malefic Mars is also placed in the ninth house of the same horoscope in the sign of Sagittarius, the native under the combined effect of all these malefic planets may have to face serious disturbances in his marriage, by virtue of such extramarital affair being disclosed to his wife. Such malefic combination of retrograde Venus, Jupiter and let's say Rahu can also break the marriage of this native after much drama, if there is no other planetary combination in the horoscope of this native which is benefic and which tries to save his marriage. For instance, the presence of a combination of benefic Moon and benefic Saturn in the seventh house of the same horoscope in the sign of Libra can still save the marriage of this native, despite the turbulence caused by such extramarital affair of the native.

On the other hand, if there is no such combination in the seventh house of this horoscope, malefic retrograde Venus, Jupiter and Rahu are placed in the ninth house of this horoscope in the sign of Sagittarius and malefic Mercury or malefic Mars is placed in the second house of this horoscope in the sign of Taurus, the native under the combined effect of all these malefic planets may get divorced from his wife and he may get married to the woman with whom he had an extramarital affair. Apart from this, malefic retrograde Venus in the ninth house of a horoscope can cause many other types of problems related to the marriage of the native under its influence, as well as those related to many other spheres of his life, some of which have been already mentioned. As always, the type of bad results and the quantum of those bad results may be different in case of different natives, depending on the type and strength of this placement as well as depending on the overall tone of the horoscopes of these natives.

Retrograde Venus in 10th House

When positive in nature, retrograde Venus placed in the tenth house of a horoscope can bless the native with good results related to his marriage, profession, finances, reputation, fame and many other spheres of his life. Accordingly the natives under this influence may witness good results related to some of these spheres of their lives where the type and quantum of these results can be different in case of different natives, depending on the type and strength of this placement as well as depending on the overall tone of the horoscopes of these natives. Since tenth house of a horoscope primarily deals with the professional sphere of the native, the presence of such benefic influence in the tenth house of horoscope can bless the native with good results through almost any possible profession in the world. Therefore, the natives under the effect of this benefic influence may achieve success through almost any professional field, depending on their overall horoscopes.

Some natives under this benefic influence may have interest in some creative abilities or talents like singing, dancing, acting, photography, music composing and other such creative fields and accordingly they may follow one such creative field as a long lasting hobby or as a profession, depending on their overall horoscopes. For example, the presence of benefic retrograde Venus in the tenth house of a horoscope in the sign of Pisces can make the native interested in acting, music composing or dancing and accordingly the native may follow one or more than one of these activities as his passion, right from a young age. If benefic Sun is also present in the tenth house of the same horoscope in the sign of Pisces along with benefic retrograde Venus, the native may become more interested in dancing and accordingly he may start taking dance lessons or he may start learning various types of dances, by any other means available to him, from his young age.

This native may become a good and passionate dancer but the combined effect of these two benefic planets may not be sufficient to make the native a professional dancer and more positive influence may be required from his horoscope. For instance, if benefic Moon or benefic Jupiter is also placed in the tenth house of the same horoscope in the sign of Pisces along with benefic retrograde Venus and benefic Sun, the native under the combined effect of these three planets say benefic Venus, Sun and Moon may become a very good dancer and he may win some dance competitions also. The native under the native under the combined influence of these benefic planets may become a professional dancer and he may either start teaching various types of dance formations in a well reputed dance institute or he may start his own dance school where he may teach other people, the art of dancing.

Though the combined effect of these three benefic planets may bless the native with good amount of success through such profession of dance teacher, the presence of some other positive planets in the horoscope of this native may further improve this equation and the native may gain more success. For instance, if benefic Rahu is placed in the eleventh house of this horoscope in the sign of Aries, the native under the combined effect of such benefic retrograde Venus, Sun, Moon and Rahu may earn even more money and recognition through this profession and apart from having his own dance academy, he may also start offering his services as a choreographer for dancing events and dance competitions. At the same time, if benefic Mercury is present in the ninth house of the same horoscope in the sign of Aquarius, the native under the combined influence of all these benefic planets may get a chance to choreograph for some music videos or even for some movies.

Hence the native under the combined influence of these benefic planets may become a choreographer and he may earn good amount of money and fame under this profile. If benefic Jupiter is also present in the eleventh house of this horoscope in the sign of Aries along with benefic Rahu, the native under the combined effect of such benefic retrograde Venus and all other benefic planets already mentioned in this example may witness great results as a professional choreographer or dance director. The native may now become a famous chorographer who may start by doing some music videos but who may soon become a well recognized face in a big movie industry. Hence the native may become a famous dancer and choreographer and he may earn great amount of fame, money, success and recognition through this profession. As more positive influences add to this equation, the native under the effect of all these influences may not only achieve more success and fame, but he may also receive some formal awards for some works of his choreography, provided his overall horoscope allows it.

However if benefic retrograde Venus is placed in the tenth house of the same horoscope in the sign of Pisces and instead of benefic Sun and benefic Moon, a combination of benefic Moon and benefic Rahu is present in the tenth house of this horoscope, the native under the combined effect of these benefic planets may become an actor instead of becoming a dancer. Such native may earn good amount of success and fame as a lead actor and if a combination of benefic Jupiter and benefic Mercury is placed in the eleventh house of the same horoscope in the sign of Aries, the native under the combined effect of all these benefic planets may earn very good amount of fame and money as an actor. As more and more positive influences keep adding to this horoscope, the native under the combined influence of all these benefic influences may achieve even more success as an actor.

Some natives under the effect of this benefic influence may also follow the field of journalism and accordingly they may fit into various profiles under the same professional sphere, depending on the type and strength of this benefic influence, as well as depending on their overall horoscopes. For example, the presence of benefic retrograde Venus in the tenth house of a horoscope in the sign of Leo can make the native interested in politics, journalism, sports or in some other such activity and accordingly the native may have very good interest in following one of these fields as his full time profession. However this benefic influence on its own is not capable of blessing the native with much success in any one of these fields, in most cases, and more support may be required from the horoscope. If benefic Saturn or benefic Mercury is present in the first or tenth house of the same horoscope, the results may improve and the native may start following a profession in some type of journalism depending on the presence of benefic Saturn or benefic Mercury in one of the already mentioned houses of his horoscope.

For example, if benefic Saturn is placed in the first house of this horoscope in the sign of Scorpio when benefic retrograde Venus is placed in the tenth house of this horoscope in the sign of Leo, the native may become a journalist and he may achieve good amount of success through this profession. At the same time, if benefic Mars is placed in the fourth house of this horoscope in the sign of Aquarius, the native under the combined effect of all these benefic planets may become a well recognized journalist who may become known for his reporting on crime as well as for his reporting on controversial political matters. The presence of benefic Rahu in the first house of this horoscope in the sign of Scorpio along with benefic Saturn may add much more energy to this equation and accordingly the equation may improve.

The native under the combined effect of such benefic retrograde Venus, Saturn, Mars and Rahu in the already mentioned houses of his horoscope may become a journalist who may want to rise to a very high level either though the field of journalism or through the field of politics and if there are some supportive influences present in his horoscope, he may even achieve one or both of these goals. For instance, the presence of a combination of benefic Mercury and benefic Sun in the seventh house of this horoscope in the sign of Taurus can supply the extra amount of energy that this native needs and accordingly the native may gain a position of advantage in one of these fields. The native under the combined effect of all these planets may either achieve a post of high authority in a well established newspaper or news channel or he may also gain some position of advantage through a political party.

It means that such native may either become the chairperson of some trust or board owned by the government where such post may be offered to him by the ruling political party, or he may become a member of a state assembly or even a member of parliament of a country by virtue of his connections with a well established political party of that country. If benefic Moon is present in the eight house of this horoscope in the sign of Gemini, the native under the combined effect of such benefic retrograde Venus in tenth house and all other benefic planets mentioned in this example may achieve very good amount of fame and recognition for his investigative journalism, where his field of specialization for such investigative journalism may obviously be the field of politics.

As more positive influences keep adding to this horoscope and as more favorable time periods visit this native, he may achieve even more through this field of journalism. For instance, if benefic Jupiter is present in the ninth house of this horoscope in the sign of Cancer, the native under the combined effect of all these planets may either become the owner of a well known newspaper or news channel, or such native may become a minister in the national government, by virtue of his connections with a well established political party of his country.

Some other natives under the effect of such benefic influence may become interested in the study and practice of law and accordingly they may pursue this field as their field of profession, if their overall horoscope allows it. For example, the presence of benefic retrograde Venus in the tenth house of a horoscope in the sign of Aries can make the native interested in the study and practice of law and if there are other benefic combinations present in the horoscope of this native, he may become a professional lawyer. The presence of benefic Sun and benefic Mars in the sixth house of this horoscope in the sign of Sagittarius may do the needful and accordingly the native under the combined effect of these benefic planets may become a professional lawyer after completing his studies in law. The combined effect of these three benefic planets is not only capable of making the native a professional lawyer, but this benefic combination can also render good amount of success to him as a lawyer, and especially as a criminal lawyer.

The native who becomes a lawyer under the benefic effect of these three planets is likely to be known as a lawyer who brings high energy to the courtrooms as well as to his trials and who leaves no stone unturned in order to win his case, though he may go overboard and shout sometimes rather than going with logics. However if benefic Mercury is also present in the sixth house of the same horoscope in the sign of Sagittarius, the native under the combined influence of such benefic retrograde Venus in the tenth house and a combination of benefic Sun, Mars and Mercury in the sixth house of his horoscope may become an even better and an even more successful lawyer. Such native may not only put in very good amount of energy to his cases, but he may also be very good with facts and logics and as a result, he may win a high percentage of his cases, which means he may become a very successful lawyer and he may be counted among the top lawyers of his genre, in his city as well as in his state.

This equation can change and become even better if benefic Moon is placed in the ninth house of the same horoscope in the sign of Pisces as such benefic Moon can add much more positivity to this already positive equation. Accordingly the native under the combined effect of all these benefic planets may either become a very successful and famous criminal lawyer of his country or he may get elevated to the post of a judge, in a higher court of law. At the same time, if benefic Rahu is also present in the tenth house of this horoscope in the sign of Aries along with benefic retrograde Venus, or it is present in the ninth house of this horoscope in the sign of Pisces along with benefic Moon, the native under the combined effect of these benefic planets may either become one of the top lawyers of his country or he may get elevated to the post of a judge, in the highest court of law of his country. As more positive factors add to this equation, the native under the combined effect of all these benefic planets may witness even better results through the field of law.

On the other hand, malefic retrograde Venus placed in the tenth house of a horoscope can trouble the native with problems in many spheres of his life including his profession, marriage, reputation, finances and some other spheres of his life. Accordingly the natives suffering from this malefic influence may have to experience bad results which may be of different type and different quantum, depending on the type and strength of this malefic influence, as well as depending on the overall tone of the horoscopes of these natives. This malefic influence may be especially very bad for the professional sphere of the native and accordingly the native under the effect of his malefic influence may have to suffer the most on the front of their profession. Some of these natives may have to experience difficulties in establishing themselves professionally and they may not be able to get stable professions till late or very late in their lives whereas some other such natives may have to face losses, problems, setbacks, bad reputation, court cases and even imprisonment, depending on their overall horoscopes.

For example, whereas the presence of benefic retrograde Venus in the tenth house of a horoscope in the sign of Aries can bless the native with very good results through the field of law as well as through many other fields of profession, the presence of malefic retrograde Venus in the tenth house of horoscope in the sign of Aries can cause problems in the professional sphere of the native. Accordingly the native under the effect of this malefic influence may not be able to establish in his profession in a proper way and he may have to either keep doing some job which he doesn't like at all or which doesn't pay him according to his qualifications; or he may have to keep changing his job after every year or two. Such native may find unfavorable circumstance in his job place and he may become a victim of office politics in many of his jobs due to which he may have to face many problems before he gets out of such job finally, and finds another job.

At the same time, if malefic Saturn is also placed in the tenth house of this horoscope in the sign of Aries along with malefic retrograde Venus, the problems of this native may increase even more. The native under the combined effect of these malefic planets may not only have to work for underpaying or low respect jobs many times in his life, but he may also have to remain jobless many times in his life for periods of some months or even for some years, depending on his overall horoscope. If malefic Ketu is also present in the tenth house of this horoscope along with malefic retrograde Venus and malefic Saturn, the native under the combined effect of all these malefic planets may have to remain jobless for a year or even for more than a year, more than once in his life, unless there are some job promoting planets present in his horoscope.

The presence of malefic Moon in the sixth house of this horoscope in the sign of Sagittarius can further aggravate the situation due to which the native under the combined effect of all these malefic planets may have to face disgrace and bad reputation through his field of profession, along with facing the other problems which have been already mentioned. Such native may become vulnerable to office politics and enemies through his professional sphere and he may have to face many problems due to such enemies. If malefic Mercury is also present in the sixth house of this horoscope in the sign of Sagittarius along with malefic Moon, the situation can become even worse and accordingly the native under the combined effect of all these malefic planets including malefic retrograde Venus in the tenth house may not only have to face disgrace and bad reputation through his profession, he may also have to face one or more than one court case or departmental enquiry.

If there are no grace saving benefic planets present in the horoscope of this native, which act as savior of the native through such court cases or enquiries, the native under the combined effect of all these malefic influences may have to suffer a severe penalty or even a term of imprisonment, by virtue of something related to his profession. For instance, if a combination of malefic Mars and malefic Jupiter is present in the twelfth house of the horoscope of a native in the sign of Gemini when malefic retrograde Venus, malefic Saturn and malefic Ketu are placed in the tenth house of his horoscope in the sign of Aries and all other malefic planets are placed in the already mentioned houses of his horoscope, the native under the combined effect of all these malefic planets may have to face the worse. The combined effect of all these malefic planets may force the native to engage in some criminal activity or some fraudulent practice related to his profession, the native may do so, he may get caught, he may have to face a court case and he may get a sentence of imprisonment for many years, by virtue of the court decision going against him.

Retrograde Venus in 11th House

When benefic in nature, retrograde Venus placed in the eleventh house of a horoscope can bless the native under its influence with good results related to marriage, profession, finances, reputation, fame, luxuries, friends and many other spheres of his life. Accordingly different natives benefitting from this positive influence may come across good results in different spheres of their lives where such results can be different in type and in quantum, depending on the type and strength of this benefic influence, as well as depending on the overall tone of the horoscopes of these natives. Such benefic influence in the eleventh house of a horoscope may be especially very good when it comes to bless the native with professional success, money and a life of luxuries and accordingly many natives benefitting from it may witness these results.

The presence of such benefic retrograde Venus in the eleventh house of a horoscope can render professional success to the native through a large number of professions and the type of profession chosen by a native under this benefic influence depends on the overall horoscope of such native. For example, the presence of benefic retrograde Venus in the eleventh house of a horoscope in the sign of Sagittarius can bend the native towards a line of profession which deals with more and more people on national as well as on international level, which deals with the items of luxury and which may also deal with the sector of hospitality. As a result, the native under the effect of this benefic influence may get interested in one of these professions like hotel business, airline business, designer clothes, perfumes and many other such fields of profession, depending on this overall horoscope.

If benefic Saturn is placed in the tenth house of the same horoscope in the sign of Scorpio, the native under the combined effect of these two benefic planets may become interested in airline industry and accordingly he may start working in this industry in a profile which is decided by the overall tone of his horoscope. The presence of benefic Rahu in the tenth house of this horoscope in the sign of Scorpio can further change the equation and accordingly the native under the combined effect of all these benefic planets may get a post of good visibility as well as that of good authority in some airline. Such native may not only earn good amount of money through this job, but he may also get a good number of other benefits also, which can bless him with a life of luxury.

At the same time, if benefic Mars is placed in the ninth house of this horoscope in the sign of Libra, this native may be destined to get something even bigger and accordingly the native under the combined effect of all these benefic planets may plan of doing something big and something of his own. The addition of such benefic Mars can open more possibilities here and accordingly the native under the combined effect of such benefic retrograde Venus, Saturn, Rahu and Mars in the already mentioned houses of the horoscope may become the owner of a business which deals with airlines, hotel industry or some other such business though he may need more support from his horoscope, in order to achieve very good amount of success through one such business.

The presence of a combination of benefic Sun and benefic Mercury in the eleventh house of the same horoscope in the sign of Sagittarius along with benefic retrograde Venus can give a big boost to this equation and accordingly this horoscope may now belong to a native who becomes the owner of one or more than one well established business related to the industry of hospitality or related to the industry of luxury. Such native under the combined effect of all these benefic planets may become the owner of an airline and he may make good name as well as good profits from this business. Moving ahead, if benefic Jupiter is placed in the second, seventh or eleventh house of this horoscope, the native may achieve even more success thorough his profession where the placement of Jupiter can change the type and amount of success this native achieves.

For example, if a combination of benefic retrograde Venus, Sun and Mercury is present in the eleventh house of this horoscope, a combination of benefic Saturn and Rahu is present in the tenth house of this horoscope, benefic Mars is placed in the ninth house of this horoscope and benefic Jupiter is present in the seventh house of this horoscope in the sign of Leo, the native under the combined effect of all these benefic planets may become the owner of more than one business which operate on very big levels. Such native may also achieve good amount of fame and recognition by virtue of the combined effect of these benefic planets. However, if benefic Jupiter is placed in the eleventh house of this horoscope in this example when all other planets remain the same, the native under the combined effect of all these benefic planets may earn huge amount of profits through such business and he may become one of the richest men in his country.

Looking at the last possibility, if benefic Jupiter is placed in the second house of this horoscope in the sign of Pisces when benefic retrograde Venus and all other planets are placed in their respective houses as already mentioned, the native under the combined effect of all these benefic planets may gain even more advantage. It should be noted that the placement of benefic Jupiter in the seventh house of this horoscope in the sign of Leo is more likely to bend this native more towards fame, authority and enjoyment whereas the placement of benefic Jupiter in the eleventh house of this horoscope in the sign of Sagittarius is more likely to bend the native towards financial profits and enjoyment. On the other hand, the placement of benefic Jupiter in the second house of the same horoscope in the sign of Pisces when all other planets remain present in the already mentioned houses, is more likely to make the native wiser when it comes not only to earn through businesses, but also to consolidate those earnings.

It means that the native under the combined effect of all the benefic planets mentioned in the last combination where benefic retrograde Venus is placed in the eleventh house of this horoscope in the sign of Sagittarius along with benefic Sun and Mercury, benefic Saturn and Rahu are in tenth house, benefic Mars is in ninth house and benefic Jupiter is placed in the second house of this horoscope, is likely to benefit more in the long run. The native with Jupiter in seventh house is more likely to give priority to fame, recognition and enjoyment; the native with Jupiter in eleventh house is more likely to give importance to incomes and enjoyments, which means that he may earn a lot and he may spend a lot also; whereas the native with Jupiter in second house of this horoscope is likely to earn a lot and invest his incomes further so that more and more growth may be achieved. Though the placement of Jupiter alone changes in this horoscope, the resultant after 20 years of business can be very much different in all three cases. It means that the native having Jupiter in the second house of his horoscope is likely to be much richer than the natives with Jupiter in Seventh and eleventh house of their horoscopes.

Looking at another variation of this planet in a similar example, if benefic retrograde Venus is placed in the eleventh house of a horoscope in the sign of Cancer and benefic Moon is present in the tenth house of this horoscope in the sign of Gemini, the native under the combined effect of these two benefic influence may once again be inclined towards a profession which deals with the sector of hospitality. In this case, the presence of benefic Sun, benefic Mars or benefic Rahu in the tenth house of this horoscope in the sign of Gemini can bend the native towards airline industry once again, whereas if benefic Moon is placed in the tenth house and a combination of benefic retrograde Venus and benefic Mars is present in the eleventh house of this horoscope in the sign of Cancer, the native may instead be interested in hotel industry, which falls in the same category of hospitality.

Some natives under the effect of this benefic influence may also become successful in various types of creative fields like acting, singing, music composing, dancing and other such creative abilities, depending on the type and strength of this benefic influence as well as depending on the overall tone of their horoscopes. For example, the presence of benefic retrograde Venus in the eleventh house of a horoscope in the sign of Gemini can bless the native with creative abilities and such native may especially be interested in acting, singing, writing or dancing. If benefic Jupiter is also placed in the eleventh house of this horoscope in the sign of Gemini along with benefic retrograde Venus, the native under the combined effect of these two benefic planets is more likely to become an actor and accordingly he may pursue acting as his profession. Such native may find good amount of work when it comes to act on stage or even when it comes to act in television programs but these two benefic planets may still not be able to bless the native with success in movie industry.

However, if benefic Rahu is placed in the tenth house of the same horoscope in the sign of Taurus, the native under the combined effect of such benefic retrograde Venus, Jupiter and

Rahu may get a break in the movie industry and soon after that, he may start working as a leading actor. If benefic Moon is placed in the third house of this horoscope in the sign of Libra, the equation can become even more positive and accordingly the native under the combined effect of all these benefic planets may achieve very good amount of success as a lead actor in movies.

The presence of a combination of benefic Sun and benefic Mercury in the fifth house of this horoscope in the sign of Sagittarius can enhance this equation very much due to which the native under the combined effect of all these benefic planets may become one of the most successful movie actors of his time. It should be noted that the native under the combined effect of all these benefic planets is more likely to become popular as a romantic hero though he may receive recognition for some of his acting works related to other genres of acting also. As more and more positive planets keep adding to this equation, the native under the combined influence of all these benefic planets including benefic retrograde Venus in the eleventh house of his horoscope may achieve even more success through such profession of acting.

Apart from this, benefic retrograde Venus placed in the eleventh house of a horoscope can bless the native with success through many other professional spheres and the same placement can also render good results related to finances, luxuries, fame, marriage and many other spheres, to the native under its influence, depending on the type and strength of this benefic placement as well as depending on the overall tone of the horoscope of a native in question. Some natives under the effect of this benefic influence can also gain money through sources which are other than their profession, which means that they can gain money through some lottery, some game show, some inheritance, some type of gift or some other such means. Such type of gains are likely to come to the native quickly or very quickly which means that the native under the benefic effect of this placement may not anticipate such financial gains long before he comes across them.

For example, the presence of benefic retrograde Venus in the eleventh house of a horoscope in the sign of Taurus can bless the native with quick gains through some type of lottery if his overall horoscope allows it whereas the presence of benefic retrograde Venus in the eleventh house of a horoscope in the sign of Pisces can bless the native with financial gains through some type of inheritance, if his overall horoscope allows it. Similarly, the presence of benefic retrograde Venus in the eleventh house of a horoscope in the sign of Gemini along with benefic Mercury can bless the native with big amount of money through some game show, if his overall horoscope allows it whereas the presence of benefic retrograde Venus in the eleventh house of a horoscope in the sign of Cancer can bless the native with easy money that may come to him from time to time through his friends and relatives, provided his overall horoscope allows it.

On the other hand, the presence of malefic retrograde Venus in the eleventh house of a horoscope in can trouble the native under its influence with problems related to his profession, marriage, overall financial equation and many other spheres of his life. Accordingly the natives suffering from this malefic influence may have to face some of these problems where such problems can be of different type and different quantum, depending on the type and strength of this malefic influence as well as depending on the overall tone of the horoscopes of these natives. Malefic retrograde Venus in the eleventh house of a horoscope can especially prove very bad for the financial aspect of the native due to which some natives suffering from this malefic influence may have to work for low or very low paying jobs whereas some other such natives may even have to work for some jobs without any considerable amount of money.

For example, the presence of malefic retrograde Venus in the eleventh house of a horoscope in the sign of Gemini can make the native suffer on account of financial problems and accordingly such native may not be able to find well paying jobs and he may have to work for low paying jobs. At the same time, if malefic Ketu is also placed in the eleventh house of this horoscope and a combination of malefic Moon and Mercury is present in the twelfth house of the same horoscope in the sign of Cancer, this problem may intensify. Accordingly the native under the combined effect of these malefic influences may not find even a decently paying job and he may either have to work for very low paying jobs or he may have to remain jobless for many years of his life.

The presence of malefic Sun in the eleventh house of this horoscope in the sign of Gemini along with malefic retrograde Venus and malefic Ketu can further intensify this equation and the native under the combined influence of all these malefic planets may have to remain jobless or he may have to engage in labor class jobs almost for his entire life. At the same time, if a combination of malefic Saturn and Jupiter is also present in the sixth house of this horoscope in the sign of Capricorn, the native under the combined influence of all these malefic planets may not have to face heavy financial debts, but he may also have to face court cases and possible imprisonment due to the non-payment of such financial debts.

Considering another example, the presence of malefic retrograde Venus in the eleventh house of a horoscope in the sign of Leo can render criminal tendencies to the native under its influence and accordingly some natives under this malefic influence may become criminals if there are other malefic influences in their horoscopes, which promote their engagement in crimes. For instance, the presence of a combination of malefic Jupiter and Moon in the third house of this horoscope in the sign of Sagittarius can provoke such tendencies and accordingly the native under the combined influence of these malefic planets may engage in various types of crimes. If malefic Ketu is placed in the second house of this horoscope in the sign of Scorpio, the native under the combined influence of all these malefic planets may engage in crimes which are related to some type of intoxicant substances.

It means that the native under the effect of such malefic retrograde Venus, Jupiter, Moon and Ketu may become a drug dealer and he is likely to operate as a drug dealer on a big level. Such native may work for some already establish drug mafia and if there are some other malefic influences which promote such tendencies in the native; he may himself become the head of a drug mafia which deals in drugs on a big or very big level. For example, if a combination of malefic Sun and Mercury is present in the fifth house of this horoscope in the sign of Aquarius, the native under the combined influence of all these malefic planets may become the head of a drug mafia, which operates on international level. Though the native under the combined influence of all these malefic planets including malefic retrograde Venus in the eleventh house of his horoscope may experience short term gains and luxuries through such life of crime, he may have to pay for his crime in some of the worst possible ways. For instance, if there are no grace saving planets and the running times are bad, the native may get killed in an encounter with police or he may get murdered by some other drug mafia.

Retrograde Venus in 12th House

When benefic in nature, retrograde Venus placed in the twelfth house of a horoscope can bless the native under its influence with good results related to the sphere of his marriage, profession, finances, spiritual progress, fame, wisdom and many other spheres. Accordingly the natives under the effect of this benefic influence may witness some of these results where the type and quantum of these results may be different for different natives depending on the type and strength of this benefic placement, as well as depending on the overall tone of the horoscopes of these natives. Twelfth house of a horoscope is a mixture of almost all shades of life, which means that the presence of any benefic planet in this horoscope can render good results to the native under its influence in almost any sphere of his life whereas the presence of any malefic planet in this house can trouble the native in almost any sphere of his life, depending on the type and strength of such benefic or malefic influence.

Moving on with benefic influences, the presence of benefic retrograde Venus in the twelfth house of a horoscope can bless the native with success and fame through a wide variety of professional spheres and accordingly the natives under this influence may achieve success through various fields of profession. For example, the presence of benefic retrograde Venus in the twelfth house of a horoscope in the sign of Cancer can render creative abilities to the native and accordingly such native may have special talents in the field of singing, acting, music or dancing. However, this benefic influence alone may not be sufficient when it comes to produce practical results through one of these creative talents and more support from the horoscope of such native may be required.

If benefic Mercury is placed in the fifth house of this horoscope in the sign of Sagittarius, the native under the combined effect of these two benefic planets may become an actor whereas if benefic Mercury or benefic Jupiter is placed in the seventh house of this horoscope in the sign of Aquarius the native under the combined effect of such benefic retrograde Venus in twelfth house and benefic Mercury in seventh house may become a music composer. However, if benefic Mercury is present in the first or second house of this horoscope, the combined effect of these two benefic planets may bend the native more towards singing and accordingly the native may become a singer, if his overall horoscope allows it.

Taking up the case of singing this time, if benefic Sun, benefic Moon or benefic Jupiter is also present in the twelfth house of this horoscope in the sign of Cancer, the combined effect of such combination of benefic retrograde Venus and one more benefic planet say benefic Sun in the twelfth house of this horoscope and benefic Mercury in the first house of this horoscope can improve the results achieved by the native. Accordingly the native under the combined effect of all these benefic planets may achieve good amount of success as a singer and he may earn much money and fame as a singer. At the same time, if benefic Rahu is placed in the third house of this horoscope in the sign of Libra, the native under the combined effect of all these planets may achieve even more success as a singer. Such native may earn very good amount of money and fame through his talent of singing and he may keep growing with the passage of time.

The presence of benefic Moon in the first house of this horoscope may provide a big amount of positive energy to this equation and accordingly the native under the combined influence of all these benefic planets may witness success and fame not only on national level, but he may also become known on international level. It should be noted that the native under the combined effect of such benefic retrograde Venus, Sun, Mercury, Moon and Rahu may now become interested in acting also and as a result, he may also act in some movies apart from continuing his well established profession of singing. If benefic Mars is placed in the ninth or tenth house of this horoscope, the native under the combined effect of such benefic retrograde Venus in twelfth house and all other benefic planets in already mentioned houses of his horoscope may become very famous as well as popular as a singer. Such native may not only become a very popular and successful singer, but he may also become a big celebrity and iconic star of his time. As more positive planets add to this equation, the native under the combined effect of these benefic planets may achieve even better results, provided his overall horoscope allows it.

Some natives under the benefic effect of this influence may get settled in foreign countries which have higher standards of living than their own countries, on the basis of their profession or marriage, depending on the type and strength of this benefic placement, as well as depending on the overall tone of the horoscopes of such natives. For example, the presence of benefic retrograde Venus in the twelfth house of a horoscope in the sign of Pisces can get the native settled in a foreign country on the basis of his marriage whereas the presence of benefic retrograde Venus in the twelfth house of a horoscope in the sign of Aquarius can get the native settled in a foreign country on the basis of his profession. Following the case of profession for the time being, if benefic retrograde Venus is placed in the twelfth house of a horoscope in the sign of Aquarius and benefic Saturn is placed in the tenth house of this horoscope in the sign of Sagittarius, the native under the combined effect of these benefic planets may get settled in a foreign country on the basis of his profession.

Taking a look at some other possibilities, if benefic Jupiter is placed in the ninth house of this horoscope in the sign of Scorpio when benefic retrograde Venus is placed in the twelfth house and benefic Saturn is placed in the tenth house of this horoscope, the native under the combined effect of these benefic planets may get settled in a foreign country as a scientist, as a networking professional or as a professional dealing with research or analysis of some type. However if benefic Jupiter is placed in the second house of this horoscope in the sign of Aries and benefic Mars is present in the eighth house of this horoscope in the sign of Libra when the other planets mentioned in this example remain the same, the native under the combined influence of all these benefic planets may settle in a foreign country as a specialist dealing in some type of financial institute like a bank or some other type of financial institute.

Similarly if benefic retrograde Venus is placed in the twelfth house of a horoscope in the sign of Aquarius along with benefic Saturn or benefic Rahu or with both of them, the native under the combined influence of these benefic planets may settle in a foreign country as some type of scientist and especially as a scientist who deals with researches related to astronomy or some other aspect of space and universe. It means that the native under the combined effect of these benefic planets may become a scientist in some space research centre in a foreign country, provided his overall horoscope allows it. However if benefic retrograde Venus is placed in the twelfth house of a horoscope in the sign of Leo and a combination of benefic Mercury and Sun is present in the first house of the same horoscope in the sign of Virgo, the native may stay in many foreign countries for different periods of length, as an officer for the government of his own country. Such native may become an officer with foreign services department of his country and he may get posted in different foreign countries from time to time, in order to discharge certain duties on behalf of his country.

The discussion of twelfth house will not be complete unless the field of spiritualism comes in as twelfth house is one of the few houses of a horoscope which can bless the native under its influence with spiritual growth. Accordingly some natives under the effect of such benefic retrograde Venus in the twelfth house of their horoscopes may not only achieve good amount of spiritual growth and become teachers or gurus in one such spiritual faith, but they may also stay in foreign countries for long periods of time in order to convey their message of spiritualism to the people in those foreign countries. For example, if benefic retrograde Venus is placed in the twelfth house of a horoscope in the sign of Scorpio along with benefic Rahu and a combination of benefic Jupiter and benefic Mars is placed in the fourth house of this horoscope in the sign of Pisces, the native under the combined effect of all these benefic planets may become a highly enlightened spiritual person.

If benefic Sun is present in the first house of this horoscope in the sign of Sagittarius, benefic Mercury is present in the second house in the sign of Capricorn and benefic Moon is placed in the tenth house of this horoscope in the sign of Virgo, the native under the combined influence of all these benefic planets may become a world famous spiritual guru, provided his overall horoscope allows it. Such native may keep visiting different foreign countries and he may keep delivering his message of spiritualism on those foreign countries. Similarly there can be many other possible ways through which a native blessed by such benefic retrograde Venus in the twelfth house of his horoscope can visit, stay or settle in a foreign country on the basis of his profession, as well as on the basis of his marriage.

Speaking of marriage, benefic retrograde Venus in the twelfth house of a horoscope is a very good placement when it comes to the aspect of marriage of the native under its influence and accordingly it can bless the native with a wide variety of benefits through marriage. As already discussed, some natives benefitting from this positive placement may get married to people hailing from foreign countries with better standards of living and they may get settled in those foreign countries by virtue of such marriages. For example, if benefic retrograde Venus is present in the twelfth house of a horoscope in the sign of Pisces, the native under the effect of such benefic influence may get married to a foreigner and he may move to that foreign country by virtue of such marriage.

Considering another possible combination in the same example, if benefic retrograde Venus is placed in the twelfth house of a horoscope in the sign of Pisces, benefic Jupiter is placed in the fifth house of this horoscope in the sign of Leo and benefic Mars is present in the tenth house of this horoscope in the sign of Capricorn, the native under the combined effect of these three benefic planet may witness somewhat different results. Such native may go to a foreign country on the basis of his profession or even on the basis of his higher studies and while staying in such foreign country, he may fall in love with a girl from that country and he may get married to her. In this case also, the native may settle in that foreign country on the basis of such marriage and he may also achieve good amount of success if his overall horoscope is supportive, as such combination of these three planets is also capable of blessing the native with good amount of success in some foreign country.

Apart from this, benefic retrograde Venus can not only bless the native with many other types of good results through profession and marriage, but it can bless the native with many other good things related to many spheres of his life, depending on its type and strength in a horoscope, as well as depending on the overall tone of the horoscope in consideration. On the other hand, malefic retrograde Venus placed in the twelfth house of a horoscope can trouble the native with problems related to marriage, profession, health, lifespan and many other spheres of his life. Accordingly the natives suffering from this malefic influence may come across problems of different type and different quantum depending on the type and strength of this malefic influence as well as depending on their overall horoscopes.

This type of malefic influence can prove very bad for the professional aspect of the native under its influence and accordingly some natives under this malefic influence may have to face different types of problems related to their professional sphere. For example, the presence of malefic retrograde Venus in the twelfth house of a horoscope in the sign of Cancer can make it difficult for the native to find suitable profession and accordingly the native may have to work hard in order to get a proper job or profession. At the same time, if a combination of malefic Sun and Mercury is also placed in the twelfth house of the same horoscope, the problems of this native may intensify many times. The native under the combined effect of these three malefic planets may not get professionally established till late or very late in his life and he may also have to remain jobless for period of some months or even for periods of some years, if there are some other malefic influences in his horoscope.

For instance, if a combination of malefic retrograde Venus, Sun and Mercury is present in the twelfth house of a horoscope in the sign of Cancer and at the same time, malefic Saturn is placed in the fourth house of this horoscope in the sign of Scorpio, the native under the combined effect of all these malefic planets may not get professionally established till very late in his life. The primary reason for all this happening may be the fact that the native under the effect of these malefic influences may not show much interest in any type of professional work and he may simply want to pass his time, wandering here and there or doing unproductive things. If malefic Ketu is placed in the tenth house of this horoscope in the sign of Taurus, the native under the combined effect of all these malefic planets may become addicted to some type of drug, alcohol or any other such substance.

Hence the native may waste a considerable part of his money, health and time by virtue of being a drug addict or an alcoholic and he may not be willing to engage in any type of profession at all. The combined effect of such malefic planets including malefic retrograde Venus in the twelfth house can also trouble the native a lot on the front of his health and accordingly the native under the combined effect of these malefic influences may have to face serious health related issues which may surface primarily because of his drug addiction. If there are some other malefic influences in the horoscope of the native, like if malefic Jupiter is placed in the third house of this horoscope in the sign of Libra when all other planets remain placed in the already mentioned houses of this horoscope, the worst type of things may happen to this native. The native under the combined effect of all these malefic influences may die at a relatively young or very young age by virtue of drug overdose or by virtue of some other fatal disease which may be initiated and promoted by his usage of such drugs.

Malefic retrograde Venus in the twelfth house of a horoscope can also give bad results related to the marriage of the native and accordingly some natives under this malefic influence may not get married till late in their lives whereas some other natives may have to face many types of problems and troubles through their marriages. For example, the presence of malefic retrograde Venus in the twelfth house of a horoscope in the sign of Taurus may not delay the marriage of the native under its influence may it may cause many disturbances in the marriage of the native. Accordingly the native may have to witness issues like arguments, lack of trust, lack of compatibility and other such issues due to which he may have to experience a poor or very poor quality of marriage. If there are some other malefic influences in the horoscope of this native, he may have to face a broken marriage on account of various reasons depending on the other factors in his horoscope.

For example, the presence of malefic Mars in the seventh house of the same horoscope in the sign of Sagittarius can cause a divorce due to serious lack of understanding between the two partners and such divorce may be finalized after a lot of drama and exchange of heated words. On the other hand, the presence of malefic Jupiter in the eighth house of the same horoscope in the sign of Capricorn along with malefic Rahu may get the native divorced due to the fact that he discovers an extramarital affair of his wife with someone else. Similarly malefic retrograde Venus in the twelfth house of a horoscope can break the marriage of the native under its influence on account of many reasons, depending on the overall tone of the horoscope of such native.

Contact Me

All you beautiful people can contact me through the following resources.

Websites:

www.AstrologerPanditJi.com
www.HimanshuShangari.com

Facebook:

https://www.facebook.com/HimanshuShangari

Email ID:

himanshu1847-himanshushangari@yahoo.com
himanshu1847-astrologerpanditji@yahoo.com

Telephone:

0091- 98551-26123 and 0091-172-466-9161